Winds of Hope

Winds of Hope

Healing Devotions for Life's Storms

REBECCA J. HUGHES

NEW HOPE
PUBLISHERS

BIRMINGHAM, ALABAMA

New Hope® Publishers
P. O. Box 12065
Birmingham, AL 35202-2065
www.newhopepublishers.com

New Hope Publishers is a division of WMU®.

Library of Congress Cataloging-in-Publication Data
Hughes, Rebecca J., 1976-
  Winds of hope : healing devotions for life's storms / Rebecca J.
Hughes.
  p. cm.
  Includes index.
  ISBN 978-1-59669-074-5 (sc)
  1. Consolation. I. Title.
BV4905.3.H84 2007
242'.4—dc22
  2007020640

ISBN-10: 1-59669-074-7
ISBN-13: 978-1-59669-074-5

N074135 • 1107 • 4M1

Dedication

THIS BOOK IS dedicated to *Matthew, Mackenzie,* and *Levi.*
With you three, I'll weather any storm.

Table of Contents

~

Foreword

WHAT A PRIVILEGE it is to write the foreword for this book by Rebecca Hughes! I know her as a student and a friend. Rebecca's enthusiasm for life is contagious, and her commitment to the Lord is convicting. She demonstrates her love for the Lord through her disciplined study of His Word and clear explanations of His teachings. She is faithful to the church, serving in many different capacities. Her call to minister to women is focused. She wants all women to experience the same joy of the Lord and peace in their lives that she knows.

Rebecca is a devoted wife and mother who loves to talk about her family. She manages to balance the many demands of life, home, and ministry with great joy. She is a strong supporter of her husband's ministry and enhances all he does through the church. They are a wonderful ministry team as well as Christian couple.

These devotionals have come from Rebecca's heart for the Lord in the hurts of everyday life. Her faith has sustained her, giving her purpose and peace. You will be encouraged as you read each thought and hear what the Lord has to say to you today in your own circumstances. Your understanding of Scripture will be enhanced, and application to life will be easily made. *Winds of Hope* will encourage you to cling to God and His Word as you face challenges in life. More than cling, you will climb from despair to hope. May the Lord strengthen you personally as you read this book, and may He then use you to strengthen others. What a joy it is to experience the *winds of hope* from the Lord!

Dr. Rhonda Kelley
Professor of Women's Ministry
New Orleans Baptist Theological Seminary

Acknowledgments

MY HUMBLE THANKS go to the following people who allowed me to tell their stories in this book:

Margaret D. Mitchell
Jason and Tammi Brown
Dawn and Alan Kicklighter
Susan Bunton
Elise Johnson
Phil Hill
Anna Marie Warren
Denise Gaspard
Kellie Mathas
Julie Holzmann
Suzzy Czarnecki and Tami
Martha Rogers
Eileen Zygarlicke
Mary Goodwin
Steve and Crystal Williams

My utmost gratitude is offered to these:

Carrie Coley,
for your contribution to this book and
for cheering me on every step of the way

My parents, Bernard and Shirley Jeffries,
for introducing me to Jesus and
for being my umbrella in so many storms

Riverside Church and especially
the LIVEChat ladies,
for making my week, every week!

The Woman on the Edge team,
for thinking out of the box with me

Joyce Dinkins, Tina Atchenson, and all those
at New Hope Publishers, who work so hard
to spread the message

Introduction

PAIN VISITS EVERYONE at one time or another. Life lived to the fullest involves heights of love and joy, but also depths of grief and despair. There came a time in my own life when I found myself crushed under a weight of grief and scorched by the searing heat of pain. During that time, I found that the Jesus I knew and trusted is completely faithful. His presence remained in my life like a gentle wind, a wind of hope, ever reminding me that, though I hurt, I was not alone. I went on, sometimes walking, sometimes crawling or stumbling, but always accompanied by the gentle breeze of hope: hope that one day I will understand why; hope that Jesus is, indeed, accomplishing something great in me; hope that my pain is seen and understood by a God who loves me; hope that tells me I can take one more step as I walk through places I never dreamed I would go.

In 2005, my life was turned upside down by Hurricane Katrina. Even though the days and weeks following that disaster were dark and desperate, I was never without hope. I clung to the hope I knew was mine because of Jesus. Indeed, I have needed the hope He offers me—not only during the aftermath of Katrina, but also in other dark times in my life.

The way I see it, the difference between Christians and nonbelievers is *not* that followers of Christ Jesus avoid pain. They don't! But because of Jesus and the hope He brings, followers can know a peace in the midst of pain. As a follower of Christ, I can know a purpose for life, a purpose for love, and even a purpose for pain. You see, without pain in my life, I may have never known just how true God's Word is. I may never have identified with His suffering for me. I may never have intimately connected with the God who made me and loves me.

Whether you have experienced the pain of a natural disaster or you have experienced some other kind of pain, I pray that the offerings in this book will bring encouragement to you. This book contains stories of my own disaster experiences and hope-inspiring stories that other disaster victims shared with me. I pray that as you read them, you will feel the breeze of God's presence in your own life and begin to hope again. I encourage you to use this book daily over the next 60 days. Set apart a time to read one of the daily devotions, think on the Scriptures listed, and let yourself be renewed with hope for one more step on your journey.

I also invite you to sit in on a LIVEChat discussion among disaster survivors, which is included in the back of this book. The sample small-group discussion provides dramatic insights. It is an example of how survivors of natural or other type disaster can share in empowering fellowship.

My prayers and my thoughts are with you.

With hope in Jesus,

Rebecca J. Hughes

I

Peace Be Still

> *The disciples went and woke him, saying, "Lord, save us!*
> *We're going to drown!" He replied, "You of little faith, why*
> *are you so afraid?" Then he got up and rebuked the winds*
> *and the waves, and it was completely calm. The men were*
> *amazed and asked, "What kind of man is this? Even the*
> *winds and the waves obey him!"*
>
> —Matthew 8:25–27

On a hot Saturday afternoon that August, my family and I evacuated New Orleans. Running from Hurricane Katrina, one of the deadliest storms ever to hit the United States coastline, we fled to our hometown in Florida.

As our close-knit seminary community also scattered, we lost relationships with people we loved. We watched on television as Katrina devastated New Orleans and other cities and towns in the region. Having no idea whether or not any of our belongings would survive the destruction, we felt the uneasiness of displacement. Yet during those awful days, God's faithfulness sustained us.

As we drove past a church sign a few days later, my mom read aloud, *"In the midst of the storm, look for Christ to come to you."*

My seven-year-old daughter piped up from the back seat, "You mean like He did for us, Mom?"

At that moment, I realized that because of this storm, God had shown Himself to us in brand-new ways. We felt His calming presence when clothing and a temporary home were provided miraculously. As we reeled from the shock of the storm, God was walking right beside us, and our children were coming to know and love Him more.

We had known Jesus is wonderful before the storm, but now we have a deeper knowledge of how amazing He is. Sometimes it is in a storm—in our case, a real storm—that Jesus shows Himself to us in a way we cannot see otherwise. Without a storm, we would never have experienced Jesus' storm-calming presence.

Prayer: Lord Jesus, thank You for taking the storms of life and making them opportunities to show Yourself to us. We love You.

Gentle Breeze: When you experience a storm, look around for Christ's unexpected presence.

ADDITIONAL REFERENCES
Proverbs 10:25; Nahum 1:3; Luke 8:24–25

2

Noah Walked with God

And God said, "This is the sign of the covenant I am making between me and you and every living creature with you, a covenant for all generations to come: I have set my rainbow in the clouds, and it will be the sign of the covenant between me and the earth."

—Genesis 9:12–13

CONSIDER THE ONLY family to survive the world's greatest natural disaster. Noah and his family experienced and were delivered from a flood that covered the earth. The Bible story about Noah is one I've known since I was a toddler. The animals that marched to the ark also happen to march across many church nursery walls; Noah and his floating zoo are major players in the children's Bible story realm. But now that I'm grown, the aspect of Noah's story that grabs my attention isn't the "Crocodile Hunter" skills he may have possessed. It isn't even the magnitude of the worldwide disaster he experienced. What stands out most about Noah's story is his intimate relationship with God.

According to Genesis 6:9, *"Noah walked with God."* He stood out from the crowd of his day. Most people living in his time were violent. They only thought of themselves. Sound familiar? It's no accident that Noah's family was the only one to survive the worldwide flood. Noah's survival of the flood was a direct result of the relationship he had with God. *"Noah walked with God"*; therefore, he received the appropriate instructions for survival. He listened and obeyed God in everything, from building the ark to loading up the animals to determining the safe time to unload the ark once the water had receded. The grand finale of Noah's flood experience was a covenant. Noah had the privilege of entering into a binding contractual relationship with Almighty God, complete with rainbow as a reminder to them both! I wonder how Noah contained himself as he watched the first rainbow stretch itself across the sky, proudly displaying God's tender promise. How vivid the color must have been after so many days of gray skies!

Guess what? In our times of disaster, walking with God still makes a difference. Just like Noah needed God's instructions and His wisdom, we do, too, as we face the calamities in our world today. God is still willing to take us through every step. I don't know about you, but I want to know God as Noah did. I want to stand out from the crowd as one whose heart is completely God's. I want to obey as God shows me His plans. I want to get out of my boat when He says it's safe, and, most of all, I want to savor the rainbow of hope in my life brought about by the New Covenant He has made with me. As the vibrant colors of His love splash across the skies of my life, I'll have what Noah had: a life indelibly, radically, permanently redirected by an amazing God.

Prayer: *God, give me the kind of relationship with You that will turn my life upside down.*

Gentle Breeze: Next time you see a rainbow, let it be a reminder of not only God's promise to Noah but also His covenant with you through Jesus.

⁓

ADDITIONAL REFERENCES
Hebrews 11:7; Luke 17:26–27

3

Unpredictable Plans

Death and **Destruction** *lie open before the* L<small>ORD</small>—*how much more the hearts of men!*
—P<small>ROVERBS</small> 15:11, BOLD ADDED

N<small>ATURAL</small> <small>DISASTERS</small> <small>ARE</small> extremely unpredictable. Tornadoes often demolish one home, while leaving the home next door intact. No meteorologist can predict the exact path of any storm. Fires spread at the whim of the wind. In spite of advanced technology, natural disasters remain out of our control. Similar to the wind gusts of a hurricane, life often brings along situations that are completely out of our control. Children make choices that go against what we've taught them. Companies make cutbacks. Accidents happen. How do we cope when life throws uncontrollable circumstances into our path?

A few years ago, I experienced a painful situation with someone I love. That person chose a course of action that caused me deep hurt and left me to deal with the emotional fallout of his painful choice. I was so angry! After all, no one had asked my permission! I had had no way to stop the awful situation from happening, but I still had to deal with the painful aftermath. I was dealing with a situation beyond my control, and I didn't like it!

I wish I could describe to you the comfort I felt when I realized that although my situation was out of my control, it was still very much submitted to God's control. Even death itself lies open before Him. My situation certainly wasn't enough to overpower Him. He was not shocked in the least by the chaos that I faced. He had purposes to show me and truths to teach me. He had some very deep, intimate times planned for me to have with Him as I sorted through the pain I felt. God, who loves me amazingly, had total control of my situation.

He's in total control. As we trust, seek, and wait for Him to act, we can abandon our need to control, looking instead for the truths our Lord wants to teach us and the deeper parts of Himself He wants us to know.

Prayer: Father, help me relax and rest, even though I feel out of control. Help me trust that You have everything perfectly in order, no matter how chaotic circumstances seem to me. Teach me what You want me to know.

Gentle Breeze: When things seem out of control, try stopping and taking a deep breath. Slow yourself down and remind yourself that our Father is in complete control.

⌇

ADDITIONAL REFERENCES
Philippians 3:21; Job 26:2; Psalm 147:5

4

Key to Safety and Security

"You will be secure, because there is hope; you will look about you and take your rest in safety."
—Job 11:18

SAFETY—WE ALL seek safety, especially in the midst of catastrophe. We teach our children how to escape a building in case of fire. We evacuate before the forecasted hurricane hits. We head underground at the sound of tornado sirens and head to higher ground in the event of a flood. We naturally run to safety when we see danger coming.

God built within us a need for safety and security. Not only do humans long for physical safety and security, but also we search for *spiritual* safety and security. Physical safety and other types of security, such as financial security, are not enough to give us the deep, secure peace for which we long. Without the sense of spiritual security and safety, physical safety fails to fully settle us. But when we are spiritually safe and secure, even some of the most physically dangerous places become places of peace and confidence.

God created us with the need for safety, knowing that He Himself is the One who meets that need. He provides, through Jesus, the key to security: hope. Without God's hope, we cannot experience peace and security, no matter how physically safe we may be. With Christ in our lives, we may come into physical danger, but we will never be without hope. The hope of Jesus transcends our physical situations, giving us the lasting security that tangible safety measures cannot provide.

Because of Jesus, we have the hope of eternity in heaven. Jesus bridged the chasm between us and God, and the reconciliation with God that Jesus brought for us sheds the light of hope over our lives here on earth.

In Job 1:18–19, Scripture records that Job lost his sons and daughters to a natural disaster. According to verse 19, *"a mighty wind swept in from the desert and struck the four corners of the house. It collapsed on them."* Could this have been a tornado? Not only did Job lose his family, he also lost his wealth and his health. In all this, Job never lost the hope he had in God. Yes, he grieved; he eventually railed against the suffering and even cursed the day he had been born. Yet he held fast to his commitment to God. Why? Because he had hope with God—powerful hope that overcame his pain and loss.

No matter what calamity may come your way, you can have hope too. You can look around during the worst of circumstances, see the hope you have, and take your rest in safety.

Prayer: Lord, help me hold fast to the hope I have in You.

Gentle Breeze: Find an old key. Label it with the word *hope* and add it to your key ring to remind you that the key to your security is the hope you have in God.

ADDITIONAL REFERENCES
Psalm 33:18; Psalm 62:5; Psalm 71:14; Romans 15:13;
1 Thessalonians 4:13–14

5

Higher Ways

"For my thoughts are not your thoughts, neither are your ways my ways," declares the LORD. "As the heavens are higher than the earth, so are my ways higher than your ways and my thoughts than your thoughts. As the rain and the snow come down from heaven, and do not return to it without watering the earth and making it bud and flourish, so that it yields seed for the sower and bread for the eater, so is my word that goes out from my mouth: It will not return to me empty, but will accomplish what I desire and achieve the purpose for which I sent it."

—ISAIAH 55:8–11

"MY GOD DOESN'T make mistakes." Those were the first words adjuster Phil Hill heard as he approached the Williamses' devastated home in the lower ninth ward of New Orleans. Mrs. Williams met him in the front yard with an affirmation of her faith in God, even though no one could understand any purpose for the destruction Hurricane Katrina had caused.

Phil and his wife had come to the New Orleans area as insurance adjusters, but they also felt the Lord wanted to use them to minister as they worked. On this day, Phil approached the home, expecting to give comfort and encouragement to a grieving family. Instead, he received an unexpected blessing and a challenging reminder of the strength available to believers who trust God completely. Mrs. Williams knew a secret that eludes some followers of Christ: she knew God had plans and purposes beyond her imagination. She had abandoned herself to His care, making the decision to rest as she trusted God to care for her. So she stood with confidence, in the midst of utter desolation, and made her declaration: "My God doesn't make mistakes."

Indeed, our God does not make mistakes. We can trust, as Mrs. Williams did, that God's plans are higher than ours. We can relax, knowing that He sees far beyond our line of vision. We can rejoice, looking forward to the heights of joy that follow depths of sorrow. We can rest, sure that our Father's heart beats with love for us, and His higher ways are always working in our favor.

Prayer: *Thank You, God, that I don't need to understand Your ways. Thank You for being beyond what I can comprehend. I will rest in You. I will trust You and Your higher ways.*

Gentle Breeze: Look up at the sky today, imagining the distance between heaven and earth. Thank God that His ways go that far beyond our comprehension.

ADDITIONAL REFERENCES
Deuteronomy 3:24; Psalm 71:5

6

Freely Give

*"Heal the sick, raise the dead, cleanse those who have
leprosy, drive out demons. Freely you have received,
freely give."*

—MATTHEW 10:8

MY CHILDREN AND I were displaced from our home for two
months after Hurricane Katrina. The first week after the storm,
we stayed with my parents, cramming two families into their small
home. My mother is a night nurse at the local hospital. Keeping the
children quiet so she could rest during the day was no easy task. We
also struggled to provide a regular routine that would help our son
and daughter deal with the losses they faced. We wanted to give our
children as much normalcy as possible before my husband returned
to New Orleans to help with relief efforts.

Our friends Jason and Tammi Brown heard of our situation
and came to our rescue. The Browns had been investing in some
property, and one of their houses was vacant. They offered to allow us
to stay in a house rent free until we could return to New Orleans.

Along with this house blessing came more blessings, as other
friends and family members flocked to my parents' home, bearing
goods and goodwill. In two days, we had everything needed to set
up housekeeping.

From the front door of our temporary home, we said a tearful
good-bye to my husband as he returned to New Orleans. He was
able to leave with peace of mind, knowing his family had a safe,
comfortable place to stay until we could all be together again.

Jason told me later that he had been feeling led to help Katrina
victims, but wasn't sure exactly what to do. When Tammi told him
about our need, he offered the home without hesitation. The offer
did not make good business sense. They could lose rental income

or a prospective sale of the house. But they freely gave of their resources regardless of what it might cost.

When Jesus sent His disciples out to serve others, He reminded them they were to give freely of themselves and the gifts God had given them. He gave them specific instructions not to take extra money or supplies, but to trust God to provide for them as they shared the gospel. Jesus's words ring in my ears as I see those in need around me. I have freely received the gifts God has given. May you and I freely give to others in obedience to Him.

Prayer: *Jesus, You have lavished Your love upon me. Please show me opportunities to give to others as You have given to me.*

Gentle Breeze: Give a free gift today. You may have only a few pennies or a few moments, but find some way to give without expecting a return.

ADDITIONAL REFERENCES
2 Corinthians 9:7; Matthew 14:16

7

All Dressed Up

"And why do you worry about clothes? See how the lilies of the field grow. They do not labor or spin. Yet I tell you that not even Solomon in all his splendor was dressed like one of these. If that is how God clothes the grass of the field, which is here today and tomorrow is thrown into the fire, will he not much more clothe you, O you of little faith?"

—MATTHEW 6:28–30

ANNA MARIE WARREN was still dressed up after attending a formal banquet in her boss's honor. Driving home through weather that continued to worsen, Anna Marie began to hear tornado sirens. She got out of her car and into the safety of a town hall building just before a category F4 tornado hit the area. She hid with a few janitorial workers under bathroom sinks as the tornado passed right over the building. Once the tornado quieted, Anna Marie wandered out to the street to find help, only to be warned of another tornado on its way!

"So here I am in a strange place, standing in the rain, with no way to get home, and did I mention I was wearing a short formal and heels?" she said. "The more it rained the shorter my silk suit grew!" She finally found a firefighter and clung to him, offering to help care for those with injuries. "The guys gave me one of their jackets and a pair of boots and stuck me in the back of the ambulance so I could help...or maybe they were hiding me!"

The firefighters pulled an elderly woman from underneath her house and laid her next to Anna Marie. Anna Marie held the hand of the frightened woman and spoke words of comfort and reassurance. After a long, exhausting night, Anna Marie safely returned home early the next morning, thankful to be alive.

Anna Marie hadn't dressed for a disaster, but God provided the strength, wisdom, and yes, even the clothing she needed! Unexpected devastation makes us all feel unprepared and ill-equipped, but our God is faithful to provide. He "clothes" us with everything we need in our desperate situations. Look to God for the proper attire today!

Prayer: Father, clothe me with what I need to make it through this day.

Gentle Breeze: As you dress today, be reminded that our God will clothe you in His finest.

⌒

ADDITIONAL REFERENCES
Philippians 4:19; Ephesians 1:3; Psalm 3:3

8

More Than a Sparrow

"Are not two sparrows sold for a penny? Yet not one of them will fall to the ground apart from the will of your Father. And even the very hairs of your head are all numbered. So don't be afraid; you are worth more than many sparrows."

—MATTHEW 10:29–31

SUSAN BUNTON SAT on the porch the morning after Hurricane Katrina. She and her husband, Ron, had weathered the storm at Ron's parents' home near the Mississippi Gulf Coast. Their son, Ethan, had opted to stay in Lafayette, Louisiana, with some friends from the college he was attending.

"Everything was quiet, no life anywhere," Susan told me. "I sat on the porch and looked at a fallen tree. Suddenly a red bird landed on the broken tree stump and just started singing. I immediately thought of how the Bible states God cares for even the little birds, so we know He cares for us. It was a special moment."

As Susan began to deal with post-Katrina life, she held on to that special reminder from God. It brought comfort as she waited for word from Ethan and strength as she searched for somewhere to get the medication she needed. God wanted Susan to remember how much He cared for her. The little red bird had delivered a telegram of reassurance of God's care.

When we face tragedy in life, everything around us seems lifeless. Like Susan's little red bird, we can sing in the midst of the damage, secure in our Lord's tender care. We can face heartache knowing that the God who knows every hair on our heads is working His will in our lives.

Prayer: Father, I'm glad You are in control of my situation. Help me to trust You even when chaos is all around me.

Gentle Breeze: Find a quiet moment to sing. No matter what may be going on, be reminded that God cares for you.

~

ADDITIONAL REFERENCES
Psalm 139:1–6; Colossians 3:15; Philippians 4:4

9

Swallowed Up in Victory!

When the perishable has been clothed with the imperishable, and the mortal with immortality, then the saying that is written will come true: "Death has been swallowed up in victory."

—1 CORINTHIANS 15:54

INARGUABLY, THE WORST result of natural disaster is loss of life. Beyond the pain of destroyed homes, personal possessions, and workplaces is the greater pain of a life or many lives being taken by a natural disaster. Long after homes are rebuilt, the pain of losing loved ones remains.

God is familiar with death and grief. When sin entered the world, it brought death along as its awful companion. In order to defeat sin and death for us, God had to choose death for His own Son, Jesus, who willingly gave His life so that the sting of death could be removed. But the story didn't end there. Jesus also rose again! He emerged from the grave in complete victory over death. The most powerful and painful force known to humankind, death, could not hold Jesus. As His death paid for our sins once and for all, His resurrection trumped death for us once and for all.

Because of our Savior, death no longer must mean permanent darkness. Death simply becomes a portal through which those who embrace Christ's saving work will enter into unspeakable beauty and unfathomable pleasure in the very presence of God Himself. We have nothing to fear in death if we belong to the Lord Jesus. Having nothing to fear in death opens us up to fearless, vivid, passionate life!

We need to know that God understands our pain and grieves with us in the loss of a loved one. We also must know that He has the final victory over death, and that victory is available to each one of us as we choose to receive Jesus as our rescuer! We can stand today, knowing that even death has no power over us because we belong to the One who defeated death forever!

Prayer: Powerful God, how comforting to know that death is swallowed up in Your victory. Help me to live in that victory today.

Gentle Breeze: Sing your favorite upbeat song of worship. Sing in the victory over death that Jesus has provided for you.

ADDITIONAL REFERENCES
Philippians 3:20–21; 1 Thessalonians 4:13–14

Lost

"Because of your great compassion you did not abandon them in the desert. By day the pillar of cloud did not cease to guide them on their path, nor the pillar of fire by night to shine on the way they were to take."
—Nehemiah 9:19

After Hurricane Katrina, Elise returned with her uncle to her family's home on the Mississippi Gulf Coast. The once-familiar community where she and her family had shared so many memories looked nothing like she remembered. Absolutely nothing remained of the family home. Elise couldn't even recognize the neighborhood or find her way around. Gone were all the familiar landmarks and the beautiful spot that had been the location of so many family vacations and fun times. Gone were Elise's mementos of her debutante days and the last letter she received from her father before he died. Elise felt disoriented and lost.

Have you ever been there? Has life thrown a storm at you that left you feeling as though you're not even sure where you are? The people of the nation of Israel felt the same way during their wilderness journeys, but God was entirely faithful to them. In His great compassion, He sent the cloud to guide them in the day and the fire pillar by night so they would know the way He wanted them to take. God is still faithful to guide His children today.

If you are feeling lost and unsure where to go next, remember that God has not abandoned you. His loving compassion for you makes Him your best guide in times of uncertainty. Look for His direction and commit to follow Him.

Prayer: Father, I need Your compassionate guidance. Help me know exactly where You want me to go.

Gentle Breeze: The guidance we need for life is found in God's Word. Spend a few extra minutes reading His Guidebook today.

ADDITIONAL REFERENCES
Exodus 34:6; Psalm 119:105; John 15:7

Detours

*As Jesus was walking beside the Sea of Galilee, he saw two
brothers, Simon called Peter and his brother Andrew. They
were casting a net into the lake, for they were fishermen.
"Come, follow me," Jesus said, "and I will make you fishers
of men." At once they left their nets and followed him.*
—MATTHEW 4:18–20

WE MOVED FROM central Florida to New Orleans in 2004. We
had no sooner settled into our apartment at New Orleans Seminary
and into a good routine of life in our new town, than a mandatory
evacuation was issued because of Hurricane Ivan. We were missing
our families and took the opportunity to pay a visit to our hometown
in central Florida. After Ivan did its terrible damage, we headed
back to New Orleans. The already lengthy 11-hour drive turned into
a grueling 16-hour drive! Ivan had taken out the Escambia Bridge in
Pensacola, Florida, effectively erasing our shortest route home. We
had to travel hundreds of miles out of the way, and we drove long
into the night to make it back to New Orleans.

As natural disasters create unexpected physical detours, they
sometimes mandate detours in life direction. Financial devastation
from a disaster can cause the death or delay of a dream. Emotional
aftereffects can cause shifts in family dynamics. Forced relocations
due to disaster can be a relational challenge as adjustments are made
to new neighbors, new co-workers, and new surroundings. Loss of
a home from disaster brings major changes in living conditions. All
these "detours" can be overwhelming and exhausting.

As they embarked on the permanent detour of following
Jesus, Simon Peter and Andrew must have felt some of the same
trepidation a disaster victim feels. They changed their line of work
in a matter of seconds! But what if they had said no?

As we drove the winding detour roads back to New Orleans after Ivan, we got lost once or twice. We saw some charming towns and stores we'd never even heard of before. We also acquired extensive map-reading skills! We turned our detour into an adventure. What else were we to do? Complaining wouldn't have shortened our trip. The same principle applies to the life detours brought on by disaster. If turned into an adventure, disaster becomes a little less heartbreaking and a little more tolerable, and it can sometimes even enrich us. The key is to cancel out complaining. Since griping never brings a quicker solution, we are better served to embrace life's detours and go down life's "side roads" on the lookout for new and wonderful experiences.

If you catch yourself complaining about a detour you are forced to take in life, try turning the tables and looking at the detour as an expedition. Your detour may be the gateway to a greater experience!

Prayer: *Lord, help me to embrace the detours You send my way. Help me gain every last inch of learning I can out of even the most inconvenient route.*

Gentle Breeze: Remind yourself today that a detour is simply a different way to a particular destination. Encountering a detour may temporarily redirect you, but eventually, you can still reach your intended goal.

ADDITIONAL REFERENCES
Philippians 2:12–13; Philippians 4:11–14; Genesis 12:1–2

12

Step-by-Step

If the LORD delights in a man's way, he makes his steps firm; though he stumble, he will not fall, for the LORD upholds him with his hand.

—PSALM 37:23–24

I'VE SPENT A lot of time over the last few weeks struggling about what my next step should be. Is it time to step out into ministry? Is it time to give up other jobs? Where will my child attend school next year? How do I know I'm doing what God wants me to do?

I picture myself looking over a boundary—possibly across a border into another land. I want to . . . I need to cross that border. At the same time, I am afraid because where I am is safe and familiar. I'm terrified the step I choose will be the wrong one. Have you ever been there?

Life's storms and disasters have a way of bringing us to major crossroads. We are faced with decisions we never anticipated having to make, and they need to be made quickly, with little planning or information. When our world is shaken by calamity, questions swirl around us: What now? Where do I go next? How will I ever survive this? Is God telling me something? How do I know what He wants me to do?

How comforting it is to read Psalm 37:23–24 and to know that the Lord is taking pleasure in my journey of faith. He is pleased by my desire to serve Him and walk in the way He has chosen for me. Any step I take is possible only because of Him. Even if I make a mistake or my plans don't turn out the way I hope they will, I'm OK because God is holding my hand.

No matter what may come along, we can be secure because of God's presence in our lives. Let's relax each day in the peace that knowledge brings.

Prayer: *Thank You, Father, for holding my hand. As Your child, I choose to joyfully walk the steps You establish for me.*

Gentle Breeze: As you go through your day, envision God holding your hand. Allow this image to comfort and encourage you.

ADDITIONAL REFERENCES
Jeremiah 10:23; Job 23:10–11; Proverbs 16:9

Peace Be with You

On the evening of that first day of the week, when the disciples were together, with the doors locked for fear of the Jews, Jesus came and stood among them and said, "Peace be with you!" After he said this, he showed them his hands and side. The disciples were overjoyed when they saw the Lord.

—JOHN 20:19–20

AFTER HURRICANE KATRINA, our church set up a tent in the parking lot. Every morning and evening, crowds would huddle together under the tent for a meal. Under that tent, the barriers that normally divide people did not exist. Common barriers, such as social status, economic class, cultural group, gender, and religious affiliation, no longer mattered. Everyone needed the comfort of togetherness.

Jesus's disciples knew this same need after His death. They huddled together, clinging to one another in their grief. This act of gathering brought them all to one place, set their minds and hearts at full attention, and prepared them for the moment when Jesus Himself would appear to them, saying, *"Peace be with you!"* The Scripture above says they were overjoyed when they saw the Lord. I can only imagine the electricity in that upper room when they saw Jesus as they had never seen Him before.

Jesus came to our Katrina tent too. Some people met Him for the first time. Some returned to Him after long separations. Some saw Him more clearly than ever before. Disasters have a way of bringing everyone to the same level of need. In the huddles after a disaster, opportunities to encounter Christ in deeper ways are common. Sometimes the encounter happens as a physical need, such as food or water, is provided. Sometimes the encounter takes place as a hand or a hug is extended in support and friendship. In the quiet of those huddles, Jesus still imparts peace and comfort, as He did for His followers so long ago.

If you are grieving today, huddle together with those around you, savor the stillness of the moment, and anticipate the presence of Jesus. He wants to bring peace to you today.

Prayer: *Jesus, I look to You for the peace I need right now. Help me remember that when I am in a desperate situation, I have a great chance to encounter You.*

Gentle Breeze: Consider how you might be the hands or mouth of Jesus to someone in a huddle of grief.

ADDITIONAL REFERENCES
Psalm 119:165; John 14:27

14

Just Like My Father

Be imitators of God, therefore, as dearly loved children.
—EPHESIANS 5:1

DURING MY LAST pregnancy, an ultrasound gave me a peek at the baby inside of me. My little one had made himself at home inside my womb. Instead of being in the normal vertical position, he was lying crosswise in hammock fashion. He even had his little feet crossed. I couldn't help wondering what my little guy would think when the time would come for him to leave his hammock. He would feel the weight of his own arms and legs for the first time. He would be cold for the first time.

No wonder babies cry when they are born! The sudden change sends them searching for something or someone that feels or sounds familiar. I remember how both my babies were instantly comforted by my familiar voice. In times of storm or disaster, we get suddenly forced into unfamiliar situations. We are introduced without warning to a life that may not be quite as comfortable as what we were accustomed to before the storm.

Are you being pushed out of your comfort zone? Are you feeling completely unprepared to face your present struggles? Times like this give us a close glimpse of our Father's face. Similar to a baby in the womb, we get comfortable in the weightlessness of the familiar. Getting pushed out into a situation we never expected sends us searching for something or someone familiar.

When our eyes find God's face and our ears hear His voice, we realize we're closer to Him than ever, loving Him in a way we couldn't have loved Him before.

If you're feeling the shock of transition, look around until you sense God's familiar presence and hear a word from Him. Then settle into the new place to which He's taken you. Start growing, and get busy learning your new surroundings. Going to a new place with God, even when you get there through difficulty, gives you a greater ability to know Him and love Him.

Prayer: Dear Father, help me to see You in a new way. Help me to hold fast to You when I face trials and stress.

Gentle Breeze: Today, embrace the hope of becoming more like Christ through the challenges you face.

ADDITIONAL REFERENCE
2 Corinthians 3:18

15

Never a Question

I eagerly expect and hope that I will in no way be ashamed,
but will have sufficient courage so that now as always
Christ will be exalted in my body, whether by life or by
death. For to me, to live is Christ and to die is gain.
—PHILIPPIANS 1:20–21

ON NOVEMBER 6, 1977, the Kelly Barnes Dam gave way to pressure from torrential rains. As it broke, a 30-foot wall of water went crashing over the campus of Toccoa Falls College. Thirty-nine lives were lost in a few horrible moments. The small Christian college was suddenly catapulted into the national spotlight as the nation watched how the college staff and students would cope with the horrific tragedy. The surviving students and faculty of Toccoa Falls College gave thanks to God for the outpouring of love and support from volunteers. They unwaveringly held to their faith in God, despite the questions raised by many around the nation as to why God would allow such a loss to befall His people.

How did these devastated believers hold so firmly to their faith? I believe it is because they understood that faith in God is much more than a feel-good system of coping. Faith in God is much more than a one-day-a-week social event. Becoming a follower of Christ is a life-and-death, all-or-nothing, bedrock choice about the way a person lives and dies. The Apostle Paul knew this. Paul enjoyed every wonderful moment of life God gave him and was prepared to embrace death for God as well. He knew he would *"in no way be ashamed"* because he had chosen God unconditionally. He had surrendered himself as an instrument for the exaltation of Christ, whether in life or in death. Paul, like the believers at Toccoa Falls College, knew that choosing Jesus is not an insurance against pain. It is a choice to commit one's life to God in this world and in the world to come. Choosing Christ involves holding fast to Him while letting go of one's own life. One Toccoa Falls professor, asked by a reporter how he would explain to the students why God had allowed the tragedy, replied, "The question has never even come up."

Believers at Toccoa Falls College didn't doubt God because they had already embraced Him completely. They accepted whatever decisions He did or didn't make as His best for their lives. This kind of surrender seems costly, but it gives way to unshakable security, inexplicable peace, abounding joy, and overflowing life. The full surrender of one's life to Christ results in a sense of peace, joy, hope, and love that no hurricane can blow down, no flood can wash away, and no death can destroy. Paul experienced it. The believers at Toccoa Falls College experienced it. I've experienced it myself in my own moments of deep sorrow. May you, too, have the ability to rest in God. May you throw yourself upon Him in full surrender, the kind of surrender that accepts death and opens the door to amazing life!

Prayer: Lord, thank You for going beyond whatever horrible circumstance may befall me. I will exalt You, Lord, in life or in death.

Gentle Breeze: Ponder the vivid life you could live if you had no fear of death. That's the kind of life you can have through surrender to God!

ADDITIONAL REFERENCES
Matthew 16:25; 1 Corinthians 15:54–57; Romans 8:35–39

16

Clinging in the Darkness

Therefore, since we have a great high priest who has gone through the heavens, Jesus the Son of God, let us hold firmly to the faith we profess. For we do not have a high priest who is unable to sympathize with our weaknesses, but we have one who has been tempted in every way, just as we are—yet was without sin.

—HEBREWS 4:14–15

KELLIE MATHAS, AFTER waiting over ten years to conceive, never dreamed that the baby she had longed for would be born in the midst of a devastating storm. As Hurricane Katrina rolled in, she found herself at Memorial Hospital in New Orleans, a place she thought would be safe as she waited for labor to begin. She huddled with her husband and her parents in a waiting room as the building convulsed from Katrina's force. The group listened to the radio as people called the one station still in operation. Families, some with newborn babies, were calling for help, saying they were in their attics in the ninth ward, and the water was rising. The chilling phone calls haunted Kellie. Fear took over her body as she endured the horrifying night.

After the storm ended, they made their way out to try to find food. The hospital was giving one meal per employee. Kellie's mother, an employee there, used her identification badge to get the one meal, and the family insisted that Kellie eat it. Devastated at the idea of eating while her parents and husband were hungry, but knowing her baby needed nourishment, Kellie reluctantly ate the meal.

The water rose in the city of New Orleans, and Kellie knew she was no longer safe to deliver her baby there. She and her husband made their way to Baton Rouge, leaving her parents behind.

Kellie gave birth to a healthy baby boy in Baton Rouge, but after the birth, her condition began to decline. She experienced severe post-traumatic stress symptoms, coupled with postpartum depression symptoms. Kellie slipped into a deep darkness, feeling every moment as if she might die. Kellie clung to a cross around her neck, unable to express her need for God's presence, but comforted by the reminder of His watchful care. Completely alone in the whirlwind of painful thoughts, paralyzing fear, and heart-stopping panic, she wore the cross constantly for months, needing the tangible symbol of God's love next to her.

Kellie slowly recovered her life over the following months. She functions normally now and enjoys her beautiful son. Still, she remains forever changed by the dark battle that raged inside her. All of us wrestle with dark times. We endure filthy, messy moments that don't measure up to our Sunday morning image. Is Jesus still there in those unspeakably painful times? Will He still look on us with love, even though we are covered in the mire of our lives? Yes. Jesus is not afraid to get His hands dirty. He will climb right down into the pit we are in and hold us there. No need to clean up first. You can approach the throne of God boldly, and there you will find the grace you need.

Prayer: High Priest, I am desperate for Your understanding grace today. I need You to identify with me in my pain. Help me cling to You and never stop trusting You.

Gentle Breeze: Even if you are unable to verbally express your thoughts, find some reminder of God's presence, and keep it where you will regularly see it.

~

ADDITIONAL REFERENCES
Psalm 46:1; Psalm 103:17–18; Matthew 28:20

17

Relief

"Martha, Martha," the Lord answered, "you are worried and upset about many things, but only one thing is needed. Mary has chosen what is better, and it will not be taken away from her."

—LUKE 10:41

MARTHA HAD A meltdown of sorts when the stress of all that was going on in her home finally got the best of her. How well I know how she must have felt. Last week I had one of those weeks. Concerns about school, jobs, family, ministry, housework, and even more were all pressing on me. I was starting to feel frantic. Have you ever had one of those weeks?

Jesus knew what Martha's problem was. She was focused on all the overwhelming tasks vying for her attention and missing Jesus, the one necessary focus.

After a disaster, the tasks of recovery are overwhelming. Day after day, something needs more urgent attention than you can give. Jesus's words to Martha were exactly what I needed to hear during the aftermath of Katrina. Sure, I was worried and upset about the stress in my life, but Jesus's words brought relief as I realized His call is the only call I must answer. When my only concern is answering that call, Jesus can then begin to help me deal with the other stresses that clamor for my attention.

Join me in learning to leave behind the stress of everyday life, remembering that obedience to Jesus is the key to all that is really necessary for us. Like Mary, let's choose *"what is better."*

Prayer: Lord Jesus, thank You for Your gentle reminder that I don't need to allow life to stress me out. I need only to listen to You. Help me to quiet myself so I can hear Your voice.

Gentle Breeze: Listen to some worshipful music today while you take some time to focus on Jesus.

⌒

ADDITIONAL REFERENCES
Matthew 11:28; 2 Corinthians 4:8–10; Isaiah 30:15

18

 *Rest*

"Come to me, all you who are weary and burdened, and I will give you rest. Take my yoke upon you and learn from me, for I am gentle and humble in heart, and you will find rest for your souls. For my yoke is easy and my burden is light."

—MATTHEW 11:28–30

EILEEN AND HER husband were exhausted. They had been preparing for a possible flood in their town of Grand Forks, North Dakota. "Our problem was the National Weather Service [NWS] kept upping the crest prediction. We'd get a sandbagged wall erected around a church, feel safe and relieved, only to have the NWS up the crest [prediction] another two feet. We then had to go back to work and up our sandbag dike. My husband and I basically went without sleep for a week trying to save churches or other buildings. When we finally evacuated, I couldn't take anymore. I broke down emotionally, crying and exhausted, not really sure what we'd find upon our return."

Eileen and her family did return after the flood to rebuild. They endured many frustrating months of slow cleanup efforts. Their town banded together as never before, and help from all over the nation encouraged them to keep working.

In desperate times, we sometimes wear ourselves out trying to survive. Disaster can compound the difficulty of basic daily activities, and simply staying alive drains us of all energy. Possibly the most damaging effect of disastrous events is the physical and emotional exhaustion that results from the heartache of loss that disaster brings. How do we survive times of desperate exhaustion?

We must learn to rest. Even when physical rest is not an option, our hearts and spirits can rest in Jesus. He welcomes us to come to Him; lay all of our pain, worries, frustration, and grief in His lap; and leave it there. We so often carry burdens needlessly when He has already borne them for us. Our bodies respond so much better when our hearts are at rest. Let Christ carry your heavy heart load today.

Prayer: *Jesus, I come to You in need of rest. I give You my pain. Teach me how to wear Your easy yoke.*

Gentle Breeze: When worries begin to drain you today, mentally picture yourself handing them to Jesus in exchange for His light load of love.

ADDITIONAL REFERENCES
Psalm 62:5; Psalm 91:1–2

19

Guard the Door

Set a guard over my mouth, O LORD; keep watch over the door of my lips. Let not my heart be drawn to what is evil, to take part in wicked deeds with men who are evildoers; let me not eat of their delicacies.

—PSALM 141:3–4

OUR NATION HAS learned the hard way that we must be more careful about who and what are allowed on an airplane. The last time I was at the airport, I stood in a long line at security, removing my shoes, emptying my pockets, and placing my bags on a conveyor belt to be scanned. Sometimes I wish I had tight security at the door of my mouth to control what is allowed out. At times, the words that escape my mouth do damage or are useless at best. They need to be scanned, searched, and sometimes confiscated before they are allowed through to the ears and hearts of others.

Times of catastrophe bring many communication challenges. Awful words, spoken in frustration, stress, and desperation, can add to the pain everyone is feeling. Our words can do so much damage, and many times, the damage is irreversible. I want the words that come out of my mouth to lift up others, point them to Christ, and help them feel loved and important.

The Holy Spirit of God can be our security. We can ask Him to help us carefully scan what we want to say and remove those words that are dangerous or even those that have no purpose. Sending our words through God's security gate may require a bit of a wait, but having the assurance that no dangerous words have been allowed to take off from our mouths will make it worth the wait.

Prayer: Dear Father, please watch over the words that come from my mouth. Please help me speak only words that are pleasing to You.

Gentle Breeze: Take some time before you speak today to let your words be approved by the Holy Spirit.

<hr />

ADDITIONAL REFERENCES
Psalm 19:14; Ecclesiastes 10:12

20

Now I See

"My ears had heard of you but now my eyes have seen you."
—JOB 42:5

ONE OF THE bonuses of our moving to New Orleans Seminary was being able to live on campus right down the street from Margie, one of my dearest friends. Margie and I met when we were both newlyweds putting our husbands through school at Baptist College of Florida. Our friendship lasted through childbirth, financial difficulties, and ministry moves.

After eight years of long-distance friendship, we were thrilled to spend a wonderful year as neighbors and were looking forward to one more year together before graduation. The day before Hurricane Katrina, we evacuated the city together, not knowing we were living our last day as neighbors for this time in our lives.

When the storm permanently displaced Margie and her family, the Lord once again became our comfort as we grieved the loss of our time together and tried to accept separation.

A few weeks later, Margie shared Job 42 with me by phone. She explained how the days after the storm had been so full of God's presence and activity that it seemed she was seeing Him for the first time. God had provided them a home and had helped their children adjust to their new environment. God's Spirit had been Margie's constant companion, helping her handle the unexpected experience.

Trials in our lives are opportunities for God to show Himself to us. When He becomes our refuge in a time of trouble and we draw closer to Him in our brokenness, God becomes more than a faraway power. He becomes a close personal Friend.

Margie would agree with me that seeing God in a new way has been well worth the storm we have weathered. Our temporary loss has produced the eternal gain of a deeper relationship with Jesus.

Prayer: *Precious Lord, You have shown Yourself to me through my trials. Help me to show Your love by encouraging others.*

Gentle Breeze: Allow your heartaches and losses to sharpen your focus on Jesus.

ADDITIONAL REFERENCES
Deuteronomy 4:9; Isaiah 6:5; 2 Corinthians 4:18

21

Dramatic Change

As he neared Damascus on his journey, suddenly a light from heaven flashed around him. He fell to the ground and heard a voice say to him, "Saul, Saul, why do you persecute me?"

"Who are you, Lord?" Saul asked.

"I am Jesus, whom you are persecuting," he replied. "Now get up and go into the city, and you will be told what you must do."

—ACTS 9:3–6

DENISE GASPARD AND her family gathered a few changes of clothes as they evacuated New Orleans, fully expecting to return in a few days. Hurricane Katrina had other plans, and they ended up stranded in a Tennessee town. Normally, a move takes planning, preparation, and packing, but the Gaspards were not able to do these preliminary activities before this move. The change in their lives had been total and abrupt! Through the kindness of their new town and through some difficult days, they have adjusted and made a home in their new surroundings. In the months after their dramatic and sudden move, they have built a new life.

Saul, who later became known as Paul, experienced the shock of abrupt change on his way to Damascus. In a split second, his life became something he never dreamed it would be. He surrendered to the severe tactics Jesus used and gave his full attention to the Lord. Saul's whole life changed. He became a new man and went on to know and serve God with total abandon.

Sometimes God allows sudden changes into our lives to grab our attention, wake us up, or open our eyes. We must learn to accept and embrace the changes God permits, for they often bring new levels of trust, new heights of passion, and new missions to accomplish. Have you been suddenly thrown into an unfamiliar place? Around the corner from the shock of change, you will find new possibilities and growth opportunities. Look around at your new surroundings and begin to discover what new possibilities God has for you.

Prayer: Lord, help me to accept change. I want to focus on the new possibilities You have for me.

Gentle Breeze: Make a list of surprises God has sent your way. Thank Him for *all* of them.

ADDITIONAL REFERENCES
Isaiah 43:19; Psalm 112:7; Colossians 3:10

22

Sheltered

The LORD *protects you; the* LORD *is a shelter right by your side.*

—PSALM 121:5 (HCSB)

SINCE HURRICANE KATRINA, the word *shelter* has new meaning for me. Losing our apartment in the hurricane meant we had no shelter of our own. Our physical shelter was gone. The shelter of friends and familiar routine had disappeared. The certainty of knowing we were where God had called us to be was also called into question.

Slowly, the realization dawned that a home, friends, and even a calling from God are not adequate shelter. We had a real shelter all along.

When our lives were stripped bare to nothing but the Lord, we found that, indeed, He is enough. What a comfort to know that with God in our lives, we have a shelter right by our side. No matter what may happen, the security found in God cannot be taken away.

If life is falling down around you, take refuge in the Shelter right by your side. Embrace the peace available to you in Jesus.

Prayer: My Protector, thank You for being ever present in my life.

Gentle Breeze: When you step into your home today, thank God for your physical shelter as well as for the spiritual shelter He provides.

ADDITIONAL REFERENCES
Proverbs 2:8; Philippians 4:7; Matthew 7:24–25

23

Live on Purpose

Be very careful, then, how you live—not as unwise but as wise, making the most of every opportunity, because the days are evil.

—EPHESIANS 5:15–16

ONE DEAR FRIEND taught me to apply Ephesians 5:15–16 when he challenged my husband and me to begin *living on purpose.* Living on purpose means to live carefully—to deliberately choose to make the most of life, its relationships, challenges, and pleasures. Living on purpose helped heal a terrible wound in our marriage. We deliberately began to do what we knew would please the other. For example, knowing I love to read, my husband thoughtfully chose a book for me and cared for our daughter so I could relax and enjoy the book. And instead of complaining about the way my husband prefers to have his shirts folded, I learned to fold them his way. Our purposeful care for each other has resulted in renewed love and happiness.

Disasters can send us into emergency mode. Life can become a series of interruptions, decisions, and desperate attempts to cope with the stress of catastrophe. It's easy to forget our purpose when we are so distressed. Don't let the pain of disaster distract you from living on purpose, from purposefully choosing to serve and love those around you.

The Bible does not promise solutions will magically come our way. Instead, God instructs us to live carefully, as wisely as possible. This means many things: It means deliberately sharing with those around us. It means no more wondering where the magic has gone in our marriage, but deliberately and purposefully doing something magical for our spouse. It means purposefully making the most of the opportunities we now have with our children instead of wondering where the time went when they turn 18.

Purposeful living is God's way of letting us do our part to make the most of the life He gives us in the present.

Prayer: Lord, help me to honor You by living my life carefully.

Gentle Breeze: Ask the Lord to show you an area in your life in which you can begin living on purpose.

ADDITIONAL REFERENCES
Exodus 15:26; Romans 12:17; 1 Corinthians 3:10

24

Be Smart and Forgive

The reason I wrote you was to see if you would stand the test and be obedient in everything. If you forgive anyone, I also forgive him. And what I have forgiven—if there was anything to forgive—I have forgiven in the sight of Christ for your sake.

—2 Corinthians 2:9–10

IN THIS SCRIPTURE, Paul sounds like a coach giving a pep talk to his team. Can you picture him pacing back and forth as if he were in the locker room letting them have it! Though quarrels were getting in the way, Paul had a plan of action to teach the church at Corinth. Paul understood that one of Satan's favorite tools is to use distraction through quarrels or disagreements. When we are focused on our differences and distracted by the annoyances of others, then we are outwitted by the enemy.

Any time a major disaster occurs, we see this principle portrayed in the media. Accusations fly, complaints are shouted, opinions are expressed, and a vile blame game begins. Paul's solution was to forgive. Forgive what needs to be forgiven. Forgive with others and apart from others. Forgive even when there may be nothing to forgive. Paul wanted to make sure his heart held nothing against anyone. Not forgiving allows the enemy a place on the team, and Paul was pointed about not giving the enemy a chance, not allowing him a foothold.

What if we applied Paul's method in times of upset and alarm? Can you imagine how much more quickly we could recover from disaster if no time were wasted on the exchange of nasty words? Imagine the peace that could be experienced in times of recovery if forgiveness were to replace flaring tempers and angry accusations!

Are you getting sick of other people around you? Are you fuming at certain persons for something they have done to you or something they did not do? Be aware of Satan's schemes. Forgive, forgive again, and forgive some more! Do not let the enemy get a foothold in your life to distract you from focusing on the task set before you.

Prayer: *Loving God, thank You for forgiving me. Please help me to stay ahead of the enemy by forgiving others when they hurt me.*

Gentle Breeze: If you need to forgive someone, take the first step in the process of forgiveness by determining to forgive today.

ADDITIONAL REFERENCES
Colossians 3:13; Mark 11:25; Luke 6:37

25

Passing the Test

*I know what it is to be in need, and I know what it is
to have plenty. I have learned the secret of being content
in any and every situation, whether well fed or hungry,
whether living in plenty or in want. I can do everything
through him who gives me strength.*
—Philippians 4:12–13

THE UNITED STATES military has come up with its own test for contentment. This test is called the MRE: Meal Ready to Eat. MREs are often the sustenance for soldiers, relief workers, and victims after natural disasters. They come in a shiny silver package, and they last forever. This space-age technology allows freeze-dried macaroni and cheese to magically come to life by simply adding water. MREs are even self-heating, but alas, they sometimes lack in the taste and consistency department. The MRE can be a difficult test of contentment for someone accustomed to regular food eaten from a plate in the company of family and friends. An individual able to enjoy the MRE has passed the contentment test with flying colors!

Paul knew all about contentment tests. He had enjoyed times of plenty, and he had experienced times of poverty. He knew how it felt to be well liked, and he knew how it felt to be hated. Paul had mastered a steady confidence in Jesus that gave him the ability to cheerfully accept whatever circumstances came his way. You and I can have this same confidence. We can also do everything through Jesus, who makes His strength available to us today.

What is testing your contentment right now? Look to Jesus to help you face your situation with a peaceful, contented heart.

Prayer: Jesus, You are all I need to live a life of happy contentment. Please strengthen me today.

Gentle Breeze: When you encounter a contentment challenge, tap into Christ's strength to help you pass the test.

ADDITIONAL REFERENCES
Proverbs 19:23; Job 36:11; Hebrews 13:5

26

Written in Stone

Because the Sovereign LORD helps me, I will not be disgraced. Therefore have I set my face like flint, and I know I will not be put to shame.

—ISAIAH 50:7

STEVE AND CRYSTAL Williams moved back to the campus of New Orleans Seminary in July 2006, one year after they had moved to seminary the first time. I met Crystal right after their first move in; we both were trying to entertain our preschoolers on the playground. We talked excitedly about God's call on our lives, about "taking the plunge" of moving to seminary, and about the new baby Crystal was expecting. After a difficult delivery of her first child, Crystal had not easily become pregnant, and she was thrilled to be carrying another baby. Hurricane Katrina hit about a month later, ruining most of their possessions and sending Crystal and Steve back to their hometown after only two short months in New Orleans.

A few weeks later, we received a call from Steve with the devastating news that the baby in Crystal's womb had died. Baby Ethan was already with Jesus when Crystal delivered him the next day. The suffering Crystal and Steve endured was enough to make anyone give up, but they doggedly kept on clinging to God and His call. Though many people questioned their decision, they moved to New Orleans again as soon as seminary housing was available. And they continue to press on toward the goal Christ had placed in their hearts, in spite of unspeakable pain and loss.

Jesus Himself had this fierce determination. He faced the cross, knowing that the victory would ultimately be His. Living a life sold out to God can involve pain and sacrifice, but always with the blessed guarantee of His love, help, and presence. We can set our faces like flint, unshakable in our determination to follow Christ. No matter how circumstances appear to those around us, we will never be put to shame. Our God has already overcome! Don't be afraid to carve your commitment to Jesus in stone. His faithfulness never fails.

Prayer: *Jesus, I commit to You with a permanent, firm, indelible commitment. Help me cling to You no matter what may challenge my faith.*

Gentle Breeze: Write the name "Jesus" on a large stone with permanent marker. Place it where it can remind you of the permanence of your commitment to Christ.

ADDITIONAL REFERENCES
Psalm 119:112; Job 13:15

 *Refreshed*

He restores my soul. He guides me in paths of righteousness for his name's sake.

—Psalm 23:3

HAVE YOU EVER wished life were like an Internet page that could be refreshed? If something were to go wrong, you could simply click *refresh* and start again! Enduring a natural disaster and all its emotional, mental, and physical aftereffects is exhausting. If only there were a refresh button during those times.

When I am in that stressed-out state in which tears are never far from the surface and getting out of bed is a struggle, God is there to remind me that He is my source of strength. He renews my life.

When those telltale signs appear to let me know I'm getting too weary, refreshing strength and comfort are as near as God. Receiving them is a simple matter of turning aside and spending some time with Him. So maybe I do have a refresh button.

I am discovering that there are certain times in my life when that refresh button needs to be clicked more often. I'm headed for that heavenly refresh button now. Will you give it a try?

Prayer: Lord, forgive me when I forget to come to You for refreshing strength. Thank You for always being available to me.

Gentle Breeze: In the most stressful part of your day, remember to draw strength from God.

ADDITIONAL REFERENCES
Psalm 103:5; Isaiah 40:31; 2 Corinthians 4:16

Protective Father

He will cover you with his feathers, and under his wings you will find refuge; his faithfulness will be your shield and rampart.

—PSALM 91:4

DAWN AND ALAN Kicklighter waited out Hurricane Charley in their bedroom, huddling their three frightened children together. They suddenly heard crashing and felt the house shake. The Kicklighters prayed for protection for their children and kept everyone together under blankets. After the storm quieted a little, they surveyed the damage. Two huge oak trees had been torn out of the ground, and one had fallen on the garage of the house.

During frightening experiences, parents naturally gather children together for protection. They do everything in their power to reassure their little ones. Children know to cling to their parents for a feeling of security during sad or painful times.

Our Father God offers this kind of protection and reassurance to us. When we are hurt and frightened, God holds out His arms as a loving parent would. He welcomes us in, offering His protection, love, and comfort. We need only to run to Him as children and gather in the security of His arms. As a child of God, you know where to go when you are afraid. Run to Him today.

Prayer: Father, hide me under Your wings. I need a refuge today.

Gentle Breeze: If you feel stressed or afraid, make a decision to seek comfort in your Father God.

ADDITIONAL REFERENCES
Job 5:11; Psalm 4:8

29

Send Me!

Then I heard the voice of the Lord saying, "Whom shall I send? And who will go for us?" And I said, "Here am I. Send me!"

—Isaiah 6:8

IN SEMINARY CLASS, I spent a month studying Isaiah 6:1–8. What continued to fascinate me was Isaiah's reaction to his vision of the Lord.

Once Isaiah saw the Lord, he immediately desired to be right and clean before God. And once he heard the Lord's voice asking, *"Whom shall I send? And who will go for us?"* he was compelled to cry out in obedience, *"Here am I. Send me!"* There was no thinking about it, no looking back, no wondering what it would cost. All Isaiah could say in response to this amazing God was, "Yes!"

The summer I was 15 years old, my boyfriend and I had broken up, and my teenage heart was hurting. I had known Christ as my Savior for several years, and my painful experience had caused me to seek Him for comfort. When youth camp week arrived, I was ready to hear what God had to say. In an unforgettable moment, God clearly spoke to me, letting me know He wanted me to serve Him in ministry for the rest of my life. That night, without a second thought, I said yes to God, and my life has never been the same. Having heard God's message for me, I was forever changed.

My original yes eventually led to the decision to move to New Orleans Seminary one year before Hurricane Katrina turned that city upside down. Even through the painful circumstances, God's unmistakable movement in my life has been thrilling! Since I first answered His call, I have never regretted saying yes to Him.

Our God is wonderful, holy, worthy, and completely beyond our imagination. A good look at Him causes me to want nothing more than His way and to desperately throw myself at His feet and beg Him to send *me*, use me, take all of me. This is ultimate freedom and passion and absolute bliss. I dare you today to take a long, hard look at God. See Him, hear what He is saying to you, and watch your spirit respond to Him in this amazing magnetic compulsion: *"Here am I. Send me!"*

Prayer: *God, You are so wonderful. I want to say yes to You. I want to be used by You.*

Gentle Breeze: Look for opportunities to express your love to God by serving Him.

ADDITIONAL REFERENCES
Joshua 24:15; Psalm 2:11; Psalm 72:11

30

Amazing Grace

But because of his great love for us, God, who is rich in mercy, made us alive with Christ even when we were dead in transgressions—it is by grace you have been saved.
—EPHESIANS 2:4–5

AFTER HURRICANE KATRINA, the city of New Orleans was a war zone. Mary served the city as a deputy sheriff and was right in the thick of confusion downtown. Fear made panic a constant threat as she and her co-workers did their best to survive with no communication, electricity, or supplies. At one point, they began to hear explosions, and without realizing what she was doing, Mary began to calm herself by humming the hymn "Amazing Grace." She had no idea until later that her humming had kept others from giving up. Even an atheist co-worker told her that he almost lost his mind until he heard her song.

The song "Amazing Grace" touches people deeply. Its words recount the awe and completion we feel when we begin to understand God's gift of grace. Our world is badly broken; we all are terribly flawed. Without His grace, our lives fall apart. We have nothing apart from God's incredible grace. Christ's sacrifice was a result of God's free grace. We cannot earn grace, and none of us deserve it. In fact, we were dead to God when He decided to apply His grace to our lives.

Grace is the foundation of relationship with God. It's the difference between life and death, sanity and insanity, going forward and giving up. Regardless of your situation or mistakes, God's grace is for you. He gave it when you weren't even looking for it, and today He still holds it out to you. It's yours for the taking. Enjoy!

Prayer: Lord, I would be in desperate need without Your grace. Thank You for giving it to me!

Gentle Breeze: Our world revolves around payment for services rendered, but God's grace is free! Let yourself enjoy that free gift.

⌒

ADDITIONAL REFERENCES
John 1:16; Romans 3:23–24; Romans 6:14

31

Questions

*"I have told you these things, so that in me you may have
peace. In this world you will have trouble. But take heart!
I have overcome the world."*

—JOHN 16:33

ON DECEMBER 26, 2004, a tsunami hit Asia, causing widespread
destruction. The tidal wave killed more than 100,000 people in
a matter of minutes. Stories were broadcast of children swept from
their mothers and vacationers frantically searching for lost loved
ones. Questions and theories began to fly. Where was God? What
good could possibly come out of such death and destruction? Why
would God allow such a cruel tragedy?

Somehow, we have become convinced that God should
orchestrate our world according to our agendas and in ways we
can understand. Unless He does things as we think He should,
we often begin to question His goodness and wonder why He has
let us down.

Yet God has never promised us a world free of trouble. Jesus
actually told His followers that trouble would come. Suffering,
pain, and disappointment are part of life on earth. We may find
that fairy tale endings are not very common, and life may not
make sense, but in Jesus, we can have peace. He didn't bring peace
by removing all suffering from our world. He brought peace by
overcoming the world and its worst suffering.

Our hope in the midst of pain is found not in a God who takes
away the pain, but in a God who is greater than the pain. Beyond
the questions, doubts, and fears lies the peace of Jesus. He suffered,
died, and rose again to win us a life of peace in spite of horrible
circumstances and an eternity in His presence, where the happily
ever after truly begins.

Prayer: Lord, I want Your peace in the middle of my circumstance. Quiet my questions and doubts with Your wonderful, overcoming peace.

Gentle Breeze: Evaluate your expectations of God. Have you been expecting Him to resolve a situation when He may want simply to give you peace inside the situation? Take a few moments to pause today and allow Him to fill you with peace no matter what may be going on around you.

ADDITIONAL REFERENCES
Psalm 44:3; 1 Corinthians 15:54; 1 John 5:3–5

32

Supervised Steps

The LORD will watch over your coming and going both now and forevermore.
—PSALM 121:8

THE FIRST OFFICIAL week of homeschool at our house was the week before Hurricane Katrina. We spent that week memorizing Psalm 121, knowing nothing about how much we would need those words during our upcoming storm experience.

After the hurricane, we were displaced, and my daughter attended school so I could work. Each day before she left for her new school, we repeated Psalm 121. The words of that Scripture came alive as the Lord accompanied us throughout each difficult day.

God faithfully carried out the promise in those words. His presence in our lives was unmistakable as my husband returned to New Orleans to began relief efforts at our church and we remained in Florida. Each step of our journey from Louisiana to Florida and back, each *"coming and going,"* was personally supervised by the Lord. Knowing He was watching over us all brought unspeakable comfort.

Today your pain does not go unnoticed. The rough road you travel is under the watchful eye of the Lord. He is your ever-present Friend. Take your worries to Him.

Prayer: My Comforter, I'm so glad to know You are aware of everything that concerns me. I place my life in Your hands.

Gentle Breeze: As you open and close doors today, remember that the Lord is watching over your coming and going.

ADDITIONAL REFERENCES
Psalm 46:1; Psalm 23:4; Isaiah 49:13

33

Under Pressure

We do not want you to be uninformed, brothers, about the hardships we suffered in the province of Asia. We were under great pressure, far beyond our ability to endure, so that we despaired even of life. Indeed, in our hearts we felt the sentence of death. But this happened that we might not rely on ourselves but on God, who raises the dead. He has delivered us from such a deadly peril, and he will deliver us. On him we have set our hope that he will continue to deliver us, as you help us by your prayers. Then many will give thanks on our behalf for the gracious favor granted us in answer to the prayers of many.
—2 CORINTHIANS 1:8–11

PRESSURE IS SOMETHING with which we are all familiar. Even on an uneventful day, our normal lives bring a certain amount of pressure. In 2 Corinthians 1:8–11, Paul tells of the pressure involved on his trip to Asia. In fact, he bluntly states that the pressure was far beyond his ability to endure, so much so that he wondered if he would live.

As we began to recover from Hurricane Katrina, we wondered what the next day would bring and if we could make it through that next day. The obstacles brought about by the storm seemed insurmountable. We were homeless and displaced. Our children had to adjust to schools in a new city. Our family was separated so my husband could help with relief efforts at home. Our lives had turned upside down, producing a feeling of uncertainty that only added to the pressure.

Paul points out in 2 Corinthians 1:8–11 that great pressures happen so we might rely on God, instead of on ourselves. Paul placed his hope in God's continuing deliverance in times of trouble.

Do you feel pushed beyond your breaking point? Do you wonder if you will survive? Each pressure you face can be a stepping-stone to a deeper, stronger faith in God. Like Paul, let's set our hope in the Lord.

Prayer: Mighty God, I am so glad You are greater than any pressure I face. Help me to grow closer to You with every difficulty in my life.

Gentle Breeze: Pick up a rock sometime during your day today, and put it where you can see it or feel it. Let it remind you that struggles are stepping-stones to closeness with God.

ADDITIONAL REFERENCES
2 Corinthians 1:5; 2 Corinthians 4:8–10; 2 Timothy 3:11

34

Stopping Place

Let the peace of Christ rule in your hearts, since as members
of one body you were called to peace. And be thankful.
—COLOSSIANS 3:15

AT OUR CHOIR retreat, we were instructed to begin reading
Colossians 3 silently and to continue reading until something struck
us at a personal level. Then we were to stay on that particular verse
or idea, meditating and letting God speak to us. My stopping place
was verse 15. I began to think of how the different jobs in my life
all compete to rule in my heart. Many days I struggle to focus on
Christ as I balance the many roles I play.

In the desperate times of disaster, fear tends to take over the
throne, ruling our thoughts and lives. The reality is that fear, though
keenly felt at times, deserves no place of authority in our lives. God's
peace is what should be the authority.

The first part of Colossians 3:15, *"Let the peace of Christ rule in
your hearts, since as members of one body you were called to peace,"* helped
my struggles with focus and fear come to an end. God has called me
to peace.

I can't help thinking that the command at the end of that verse,
"And be thankful," was included there purposely. Many times I lose
the peace of God in my life, and nothing brings it back into focus as
does thankfulness.

Join me today in letting Christ rule. Set aside all that is pulling
at you. Thank the Lord for His mercy, grace, and presence in your
life, and let the peace of Christ take its rightful place as the ruler in
your heart.

Prayer: Lord, thank You for the gift of peace. Help me to make Your
peace the rule in my life.

Gentle Breeze: Set aside a few moments today to cultivate the peace of Christ in your life. Try meditating on Scripture or singing a song of praise to Him. Allow Him to soothe your heart.

ADDITIONAL REFERENCES
Numbers 6:26; Psalm 29:11; Psalm 119:165

35

The Prayerwalk

The intense prayer of the righteous is very powerful.
—James 5:16 (HCSB)

MARGARET MITCHELL, a flight attendant living on Kent Island, Maryland, when Tropical Storm Isabel threatened the Maryland coastline in 2003, was due to fly out the next day. She prepared as quickly as she could for the storm and then walked around her neighborhood praying for safety and protection. With peace in her heart, she flew out the next morning as the storm began to approach.

Margaret kept in touch with a neighbor, and when bridges opened again, she returned to Kent Island. In awe, she observed that the homes on her prayerwalk route were undamaged! Even homes right on the water's edge had escaped demise. All around, the community was destroyed, but Margaret's prayerwalk route had been spared.

Prayer makes a difference. God may not always choose to answer by granting our requests, but communication with Him changes us every time. When we pray, we deepen our relationship with Almighty God. With each conversation, we learn a little more about our incomprehensible Creator. Many times, He chooses to intervene when we ask. Pray about your situation today.

Prayer: Lord, I lay my situation before You. I bring my feelings, pain, and fears to You. I trust You to provide the perfect answer in Your perfect time.

Gentle Breeze: Talk out loud to God today.

ADDITIONAL REFERENCES
Psalm 66:20; Proverbs 15:29; Matthew 21:22

36

Life That Is Truly Life

Command them to do good, to be rich in good deeds, and to be generous and willing to share. In this way they will lay up treasure for themselves as a firm foundation for the coming age, so that they may take hold of the life that is truly life.
—1 Timothy 6:18–19

The week after Hurricane Katrina did its damage, my eyes were blurry with tears as I watched my cousin and childhood friend, Dawn, bring dish after dish into my parents' kitchen. With each return trip from her van, she brought in more—clothes, toys, and food. I shed tears of joy as I realized how blessed I really was by my family's sharing with me and showing God's love to me. I'm not sure I've ever felt so alive.

As I sorrowed over losses from the hurricane, I also experienced a childhood friendship renewed, love extended, and great compassion shown. I was witnessing the taking hold of *"life that is truly life."*

Times of pain present opportunities for doing good, being generous, and taking hold of life that is real. Dawn, being rich in good works, seized the opportunity, giving herself and me a precious experience that we won't soon forget.

Being wealthy in good works is a richness that has much more value than money and produces truly real life.

Prayer: Lord, help me to be generous with what You have given me.

Gentle Breeze: Take hold of life that is rich and real by extending God's goodness to someone today.

Additional Reference
Matthew 6:25–34

82

37

I Am

God said to Moses, "I AM WHO I AM. This is what you are to
say to the Israelites: 'I AM has sent me to you.'"
—EXODUS 3:14

THIS MORNING I was at church singing a song about the name of
God, I AM. I couldn't stop my tears as I thought about what I AM
has been to me.

When I was a child, God was my hero, a God who could do
anything. When I was a teenager, He was my friend, my confidante,
the One still there after I broke up with a boyfriend or made
a mistake. When I became a new wife and a new mom, He stayed
awake with me at night and gave me strength to forgive, to love,
and to make my marriage work. After a hurricane upset my life and
created so many unanswered questions, He provided food, clothing,
shelter, work, and the loving arms of friends and family. He even
provided the Federal Emergency Management Agency (FEMA),
which was a great help to me!

When I am serving God, He supplies unending grace for
whatever task is before me. Every day, no matter what I need, I can
call out to Him, and He *is* I AM to me. He is the One who makes my
life complete, who gives me strength to go on, and who makes my
journey fun. God can be trusted to meet my future needs as He has
met my past needs.

The descriptive name *I AM* is the perfect way to express how
God is utterly all we will ever need. The Great I AM is waiting to
be the One who fills the needs in your life. Place your trust in Him,
knowing *He is* the answer to whatever you face.

Prayer: Lord, thank You for Your precious name, I AM. Thank You for
meeting my every need.

Gentle Breeze: List five ways I AM has met your needs in the past. Keep your list in a place where you will see it often, so you will be reminded regularly of all God provides in your life.

ADDITIONAL REFERENCES
Isaiah 12:6; Isaiah 44:6; Isaiah 9:6

38

Be Still and Know

"Be still, and know that I am God; I will be exalted among the nations, I will be exalted in the earth."
—Psalm 46:10

WAITING TO BEGIN choir practice, our fun-loving group at Riverside Baptist was milling around, joking, laughing, and catching up on each other's lives. Nothing was out of the ordinary until it was time to begin practice and my husband, Matthew, said, "Let's pray."

I was taken aback by the hush that immediately came over the room. The silence was so complete it seemed to echo reverence for the God we were about to approach. It felt like the stillness after a storm, almost like the eerie quiet after the deafening noises of a hurricane or tornado.

During that choir practice, I scrawled these words in the front of my Easter music book:

BEING STILL

I love the silence in Your presence,
Quiet awe that fills the room
When Your people come together
Seeking You with hearts in tune.

For You are high and holy,
And in the midst of all our rush
As we enter Your presence,
Our hearts know a peaceful hush.

For it is true that when we
Turn to look upon Your face,
Our burdens and our worries
Can no longer hold first place.

They must bow and bend before You;
They can hold our hearts no more.
For in that silence we hear
What we couldn't hear before.

We hear You say, "I love you.
Come, my child. Sit with me."
And we respond, "Lord Jesus,
There's no place we'd rather be!"

God's existence is a fact. When we are still, we get to know He is God and begin to take in that knowledge as a part of ourselves, making it foundational to the way we live our lives.

Prayer: **Dear Lord, thank You for opportunities to be still and relax in the knowledge of You.**

Gentle Breeze: As you enter God's presence next time, let the silence echo for a moment as you quietly reflect on who He is.

ADDITIONAL REFERENCES
Isaiah 30:15; Isaiah 32:17; Psalm 131:2

39

Spirit Erosion

Not only so, but we also rejoice in our sufferings, because we know that suffering produces perseverance; perseverance, character; and character, hope. And hope does not disappoint us, because God has poured out his love into our hearts by the Holy Spirit, whom he has given us.

—ROMANS 5:3–5

NATURAL DISASTERS MAKE permanent changes in the surface of the earth. Hurricanes have a way of rearranging coastlines; floods enlarge rivers and lakes; fires erase acres of forest. In the wake of natural disaster, the landscape is left forever changed, marked by the massive brushstroke of nature. Once the state of emergency settles down, experts often spend years evaluating the rearrangements made by large disasters, discovering the new design.

As they rework the surface of the earth, disasters also leave the lives of human beings altered forever. Loss and survival, depletion and recovery, suffering and healing—these experiences mold the human heart into a new shape. Trials have a way of eroding the rough edges, erasing the petty anger, and enlarging the compassionate spirit of a Christ follower. On the other side of painful experiences, we get to evaluate and enjoy the remodeling job God has done in our lives. He sometimes uses the brushstrokes of pain to add inexplicable beauty to the canvases of our lives. He paints in us the deep hues of perseverance, strong lines of character, and bright sparkles of hope.

As I look back over my painful experience, I find myself changed, as the land is changed by great disasters. I must admit that I would not undo any of my life's trials if the undoing required me to go back to what I once was: a canvas with bland color; a weak, self-made portrait that was an inadequate image of the woman God intends for me to be. In the darkest times, God has given me glimpses of Himself that I desperately needed to see. He has used heartache to take away undesirable parts of me and highlight beauty in me that I never knew existed. He has stretched me beyond where I thought I could reach and has bonded me with Himself in a deep, inexpressible way. How grateful I am for God's loving artistry in my life! He has taken me on as a project and is creating loveliness in me that I could never possess without Him.

As you emerge from a painful time, look back over what you've learned and celebrate God's artwork on the canvas of your life.

Prayer: Lord, make me into a work of art more beautiful than I could ever be on my own.

Gentle Breeze: Be a student in God's art class. Look for the lessons He is teaching and the beauty He is creating in you.

ADDITIONAL REFERENCES
Isaiah 61:3; Ezekiel 16:14; 1 Peter 3:3−4

40

Heritage

*I have Your decrees as a heritage forever; indeed, they are
the joy of my heart. I am resolved to obey Your statutes to
the very end.*

—Psalm 119:111–112 (HCSB)

As we watched the television reports of Hurricane Katrina and
the resulting levee breaches in our city of New Orleans, we began
to adjust to the idea of losing our possessions. I grieved over the
possible loss of my grandmother's Bible, my wedding pictures, my
babies' pictures, and even my favorite clothes.

As I searched the Scriptures for hope from the Lord, He led me
to this passage in Psalm 119. Hope rushed into my heart as I read,
"I have Your decrees as a heritage forever."

I hadn't lost my true heritage! The words and ways of God are
my true heritage, and, unlike material possessions, they can never
be taken from me.

I began to understand how the Lord provides an immovable
joy and security in my life. I thought the hurricane and flood had
stripped me of my special belongings, but my joy and security in
God could not be removed, not even by the fiercest of storms.

Let's celebrate the forever heritage we have in Christ!

Prayer: Eternal God, thank You for the security I have found in You.

Gentle Breeze: Carry your Bible with you today. Let it remind
you of the forever heritage you have in Christ.

◠

Additional References
Psalm 61:5; Matthew 6:33

41

My Provider

"So do not worry, saying, 'What shall we eat?' or 'What shall we drink?' or 'What shall we wear?' For the pagans run after all these things, and your heavenly Father knows that you need them. But seek first his kingdom and his righteousness, and all these things will be given to you as well. Therefore do not worry about tomorrow, for tomorrow will worry about itself. Each day has enough trouble of its own."

—Matthew 6:31–34

A WEEK HAD passed since Hurricane Katrina. We had evacuated to Florida with only a few changes of clothes, and the extent of our loss was still unknown. As I stared numbly at myself in the mirror of a department store dressing room, the task of replacing our clothes and other belongings was more than I could comprehend.

Sandi, my sister-in-law, and Glenda, her mother-in-law, kept piling clothes in the room, and I kept trying them on. At first glance, we were three women having a great time shopping together. No one could tell by looking at us that Glenda and Sandi were God's way of providing for me, replacing my clothes and even adding some accessories. Special people like Sandi and Glenda were the hands God used to replenish my basic needs.

In the midst of my need, even before I could comprehend it, God had begun to provide. God had not forgotten my obedience to His call, and He was already busy giving me the *"all these things"* of which Jesus spoke. I could relax and let God handle the rest.

Jesus's promise is still true. You, too, can trust God to provide what you need.

Prayer: Thank You, Father, for caring for the smallest of my needs as I put You first in my life.

Gentle Breeze: Thank God for the ways He has provided for your basic needs.

ADDITIONAL REFERENCES
Philippians 4:19; 2 Corinthians 9:9–11

42

Guard My Heart

And the peace of God, which transcends all understanding,
will guard your hearts and your minds in Christ Jesus.
—Philippians 4:7

MY FRIEND TIM Evans knew how to have joy in the midst of suffering. Whenever I visited him in his nursing home room, he would be smiling. Between breaths on his ventilator, he would gab about his mom's recent visit or the weather. He would joke with my children and share his collection of stuffed animals with them.

Even though lots of tubes and machinery surrounded Tim, my kids never seemed frightened. I think it's because Tim's smile overcame the scariness of all the equipment. My children could sense the peace in Tim's heart, and it set them at ease.

Evacuation for Hurricane Katrina was too much for Tim's body. He went home to heaven, leaving behind some wonderful memories and a resounding challenge.

Tim endured separation from family, loneliness, surgeries, and pain with hope and a smile. Maybe, without even knowing it, he had figured out how to allow God's peace to stand guard over his heart. At times when living a life of peace seems elusive, Tim stands as a reminder that peace is available in the worst of circumstances.

Like Tim, we can live lives of peace. Instead of allowing stress and anxiety to control us, we can enjoy peaceful rest in God's love.

Prayer: Prince of Peace, rule over my life today.

Gentle Breeze: Relax and allow God's peace to guard your heart.

ADDITIONAL REFERENCES
Psalm 34:14; Proverbs 14:30; Isaiah 26:12

43

Excellent Concentration

Finally, brothers, whatever is true, whatever is noble, whatever is right, whatever is pure, whatever is lovely, whatever is admirable—if anything is excellent or praiseworthy—think about such things.

—PHILIPPIANS 4:8

IN TODAY'S WORLD of fast-paced technology, when a disaster occurs, the entire world can visually experience the devastation through television cameras. After a natural disaster, news coverage is repetitive and incessant. In the first days after Hurricane Katrina, I was glued to the television screen at my parents' home, hoping to hear a new shred of information about the condition of our home, our church, and our friends.

Slowly, tiny bits of information would emerge, but mostly I watched the same images play again and again. Each repetition triggered a fresh flood of tears.

Finally, I could take no more. From that point on, the television remained off for most of the day, and we watched only one newscast each evening to gather new findings about our city. Instead of focusing on the news, we turned our focus to the facts we knew firsthand: We knew God was on our side. We knew He was able to care for us and the many loved ones we missed. We knew He would send us direction about when and how to return to New Orleans.

I noticed an incredible difference in my husband, my children, and myself when we stopped focusing on the constant media flow surrounding the disaster. Trusting the Lord was much easier when we focused on the true, excellent, praiseworthy truths instead of the dark, exaggerated, disastrous happenings. The peace we had known since the beginning of the Katrina ordeal was felt more keenly than ever.

Today, shift your focus from the terrible and frightening things around you to the lovely, pure truth of God. Determine to think about the beautiful and excellent things rather than the discouraging and frustrating.

Prayer: Lord, Your truth is so much lovelier than my situation. Help me keep my thoughts focused on the beauty of You.

Gentle Breeze: Controlling your intake of disturbing media images can significantly reduce the negative thoughts in your mind. Take an inventory of how much news—by means of television, radio, or newspaper—you are taking into your mind. Try reducing your intake to one update each day, enough to glean the information you need.

ADDITIONAL REFERENCES
Psalm 34:14; Psalm 37:37; Psalm 85:8–10; Isaiah 26:3

44

An Error?

A joyful heart makes a face cheerful, but a sad heart [produces] a broken spirit.
—PROVERBS 15:13 (HCSB)

JULIE HOLZMANN EXPERIENCED a California earthquake. "I was in the middle of typing up an email when the earthquake hit and we lost power," she said. "I noticed a few days later, there was a message in my email stating that an error occurred while trying to send the message. Some error!" Julie's ability to laugh at her situation was invaluable. Joy can be found even in the midst of terrible pain, and Julie understood that holding on to joy would greatly reduce her stress level. She and her husband giggled about "losing their marbles" when they discovered the quake had tipped over a cup of marbles on their shelf.

Inconvenience and frustration are inevitable when life is interrupted by natural disaster. The lack of everyday conveniences, such as electricity and phone service, can be irritating. We feel panic when we don't have necessities, including clean water or safe shelter. Downed trees and ruined buildings all around produce an unsettled feeling. Questions are endless and answers are nowhere to be found. Rather than give in to fear or despair, we can learn to search for and appreciate even the tiniest sources of joy or bits of humor.

Bliss can be found in something as simple as a hot shower or a soft pillow. Moments of joy can occur in emergency shelters, in Red Cross lines, and in hospital waiting rooms. Natural disasters rob us of normalcy, possessions, and even loved ones, but we do not have to allow a disaster to take all the joy from our lives. A small smile, a short laugh, and an increased appreciation for the availability of even the most basic necessities are all ways we can allow deep, abiding joy to grow and bubble up to the surface of our lives. A merry heart is the best salve we can apply to the wound created by natural disaster.

Prayer: Lord, show me humor and joy in my situation. Quiet my panic and help me see the happiness You provide all around me.

Gentle Breeze: Slow down today and look for moments of joy.

ADDITIONAL REFERENCES
Job 8:21; Psalm 5:11; Romans 15:13

45

Overwhelmed

Surely he took up our infirmities and carried our sorrows, yet we considered him stricken by God, smitten by him, and afflicted. But he was pierced for our transgressions, he was crushed for our iniquities; the punishment that brought us peace was upon him, and by his wounds we are healed.

—Isaiah 53:4–5

NINE WEEKS AFTER Hurricane Katrina, I drove through what once was my busy New Orleans neighborhood. As I drove, I stared openmouthed at the morbid ghost town around me. A suffocating feeling of sorrow settled over me as I tried to comprehend the suffering in my part of town alone. Mile after mile I drove and saw house after house lying in ruins. I knew each house represented a family's life turned upside down.

Suddenly, the understanding washed over me that this terrible destruction, which was too much for me to bear, was only a tiny part of what Jesus bore on the cross for us. In that moment, I had a new glimpse of the sacrifice that He made for me. My own sorrow and sin is, at times, too much for me to stand. Jesus shoulders not only my suffering but also that of every family represented by the ruined homes I saw.

The trials we go through help us to identify more with Jesus and His suffering for us. When we experience deep pain, we have a glimpse of His deep sacrifice for us. It takes an overwhelming love to swallow up overwhelming pain. Understanding His great love for us expands our love for Him. Let's thank God for His unbelievable gift!

Prayer: Jesus, *Your sacrifice means so much to me. Thank You for identifying with my suffering.*

Gentle Breeze: Spend a few extra moments thanking God for the gift of His Son, Jesus.

ADDITIONAL REFERENCES
Psalm 119:50; Jeremiah 15:15; Romans 5:3

46

The Highest Power

"Listen! Listen to the roar of his voice, to the rumbling that comes from his mouth. He unleashes his lightning beneath the whole heaven and sends it to the ends of the earth. After that comes the sound of his roar; he thunders with his majestic voice. When his voice resounds, he holds nothing back. God's voice thunders in marvelous ways; he does great things beyond our understanding. He says to the snow, 'Fall on the earth,' and to the rain shower, 'Be a mighty downpour.' So that all men he has made may know his work, he stops every man from his labor."

—Job 37:2–7

NATURE IS A powerful force. Natural disasters are grim reminders of how little control we have over nature and how minute we are in comparison to its forces. In today's world, we manage and control almost every aspect of our lives, but no one has power over nature, and no one can stop a disaster from coming. Nature's incredible force can damage, destroy, and even kill. We feel insignificant and helpless in the face of such enormous power.

We have only one place to go when nature's disasters bring us pain, only one place to turn when we are frightened by nature's destruction. We can run to the only One more powerful than nature's force: nature's Creator, God!

Nature testifies of God day and night, and the power of nature offers only a hint of His power. Yet this more powerful One, God, loves *us!* His heart yearns for a relationship with us. God's magnificent creation, with all its beauty, power, and might, has a loving, tender purpose: to awaken our hearts to our Creator's existence and to fuel our longing to know Him!

How wonderful it is not only that we can know One whose power surpasses anything we can imagine, but that His mighty heart beats for us! He rules over all, even nature bows to Him, and yet He cares for you and me. Knowledge of this creates hope. Though the world itself may come to an end, we know the One who will never end, and we are loved by Him. You and I are never helpless, never hopeless.

I am compelled to know this amazing God! I must respond to such power and love! Will you also respond? Will you accept an invitation from the Most High God to know Him more, experience His love, and ultimately see His very face? How can we resist? Earth in all its glory pales in comparison to what awaits us.

Prayer: Thank You, Lord, that You surpass nature's power. No disaster frightens You; no tragedy panics You. Your might goes beyond my wildest imagination, yet You love me. I need You!

Gentle Breeze: Let the world around you awaken your heart to God's presence.

ADDITIONAL REFERENCES
Exodus 9:16; 1 Chronicles 29:11

47

Plugged In

By Carrie Coley

"I am the vine; you are the branches. If a man remains in me and I in him, he will bear much fruit; apart from me you can do nothing."

—John 15:5

ON THAT FATEFUL day in August 2005, Hurricane Katrina roared ashore bringing wind, rain, and total chaos to many of our lives. I had evacuated New Orleans and was in rural Rankin County, Mississippi, watching the effects of the storm on TV when it happened. The power went out, and it stayed out for what seemed like an eternity.

What did I learn through this? On day four of having no power, I learned that if a generator will run a freezer and a fan, it will run a TV and a satellite cable box! I discovered that the most awful thing about not having power was *not* that I could not watch TV. I found that I was *most* affected by just how dark my house would become once the sun went down.

Without God's power, our lives are dark and hopeless. When we are plugged into God's awesome power, His light shines in and through us. This light brings hope into our lives, and that hope spills over into the lives of others around us.

Are you plugged into God's power? If not, get plugged by asking God to shine His eternal light into your life so you will have the hope that comes only through Him.

Prayer: *Father, Thank You that we do not have to live in darkness, but we can live in the light of Your love and forgiveness. Help us to stay plugged into You as our power source and rely on You in every storm of life. Amen.*

Gentle Breeze: Each time you use electricity today, be reminded to plug into God's power.

ADDITIONAL REFERENCES
Psalm 20:6; Psalm 68:28; 2 Peter 1:3

48

God Cares

Cast all your anxiety on him because he cares for you.
—1 Peter 5:7

MY DAUGHTER, MACKENZIE, and I were flying to Florida for a long-awaited visit with my family. When we landed in Orlando, we went straight to the curbside pickup area, expecting Heather, my sister-in-law, to be there waiting for us. We didn't realize she was waiting at the gate instead. Mackenzie and I stood at the curb and waited…and waited. I was beginning to go into emergency mode, thinking that Heather may have had a flat tire or been in an accident.

One hour after Heather was to meet us, Mackenzie and I decided we had to pray. Bowing our heads, we prayed, "God, we don't know where Aunt Heather is, but please keep her safe and help her find us. We don't know what to do, but, Lord, please help us get to Nanny's house somehow. Amen."

As we opened our eyes, we heard someone shout, "Mackenzie!"

It was Heather and my nephew, Noah. They had given up on waiting at the gate and had come looking for us.

Mackenzie and I looked at each other in utter disbelief. I'll never forget the expression on Mackenzie's face as we saw God immediately coming to our aid.

"How's that for quick?" I asked her.

"Oh, yeah, Mom!" she said.

How amazing is it that the God of the ages provided an opportunity to show my little girl that He does care about us when we feel afraid or worried? That lesson certainly came in handy as we faced the devastation of Hurricane Katrina. Our children expected us to look to God for help, and they did the same. How precious it is that we can share with Him not only our great, heavy burdens but also our little daily stresses.

God cares! God cares for me, and He cares for you. Cast all your cares upon Him today.

Prayer: *Thank You, Lord, for caring about all things, both large and small, in my daily life. Help me to trust You each day.*

Gentle Breeze: Talk to God about a problem with which you would not normally trouble Him. He cares for you!

ADDITIONAL REFERENCES
Psalm 55:22; Psalm 144:2–3; Ephesians 5:29

49

Do It Afraid

"Be strong. Take courage. Don't be intimidated. Don't give them a second thought because GOD, your God, is striding ahead of you. He's right there with you. He won't let you down; he won't leave you."

—Deuteronomy 31:6 (*The Message*)

MY FRIEND MARY is an officer with the New Orleans Sheriff's Department. After Hurricane Katrina, she told me the profound piece of instruction from her training that got her through the aftermath of the storm: "Do it afraid." Her words echoed in my heart as I thought about how many times fear stops me from moving forward. Mary's mantra, "Do it afraid," reminded her (and me) that the first step to overcoming fear is to move forward in spite of the fear. Are you afraid? OK then, do it afraid, but do it!

Disaster can leave victims with a paralyzing sense of fear. What if another disaster occurs? What if I lose my job? What if I can't pay my bills? What if my home is destroyed? What if I can't recover from this? Simply functioning from one day to the next can be a fearful task for those dealing with the aftermath of disaster. Feelings of anxiety are a normal part of working through the stress of a natural disaster. But, just as God encouraged Israel not to allow fear to stop them from moving into the land He promised them, our God encourages us to keep going, even in fearful times.

When we are afraid, we can cling to the precious promise that God, our God, is striding ahead of us. We can be strong and seize the courage we need to take the next step, make the next phone call, and fill out the next form. He's right there with us! He's never going to leave us.

What is it you fear today? Facing the pain of loss? Dealing with the details of recovery? Letting God see your questions and doubts?

Whatever you dread, do it afraid! Don't wait until you feel no fear. Step out in the face of the fear, and take hold of the courage found through the knowledge of God's presence in your life.

Prayer: Lord, I feel afraid. I don't want fear to stop me from believing and trusting in You. Help me to "do it afraid" and keep on walking as I trust You to be with me always.

Gentle Breeze: As you go about your day, be reminded that you are not alone. Use the old tie-a-string-around-your-finger technique to remind yourself that you are always encased in God's gentle presence.

Additional References
Psalm 56:3; Isaiah 41:10; 1 John 4:18

50

A New Thing

"See, I am doing a new thing! Now it springs up; do you not perceive it? I am making a way in the desert and streams in the wasteland."

—Isaiah 43:19

A VERY PREGNANT Tami left her home after being warned that wildfires were burning dangerously near. She and her husband, Doug, grabbed very few things in their rush to get Tami to safety. After the fires had done their damage, Doug and Tami returned to find nothing left of their home. Only charred ground remained where their home had been.

Tami and Doug worked frantically to establish a home before their baby was born. They moved into a rental home and began the work of rebuilding. The home site, what they began to call "the lot," was a place of hopelessness, a picture of complete destruction. About six weeks after the fire, Tami's mother got a phone call. Tami was on the line. "Mom, you will never believe what is happening at the lot." The bulbs Tami had planted prior to the fire were poking up out of the blackened ground! As they stubbornly grew, they stood as reminders that even in the middle of loss, God keeps giving new life. On Christmas Eve, Tami gave birth to Ethan, a precious new life springing up in the painful aftermath of loss.

Like Tami and Doug, we must look up from our pain to see God's new things as they spring up. Hopeless moments are never the way God ends a story. Hopeless moments are often God's way of making room in our lives for His new thing. Even as we writhe in the pain of our lives, our faithful God works steadily, making a way through the desert and streams through the wastelands of our existence. May God reveal to you the hope of a new thing He is bringing out of your painful experiences.

Prayer: *Lord, I want to see and take part in the new thing You are doing. Help me embrace it as it springs up in my life.*

Gentle Breeze: Plant a seed or buy a fresh plant. Let its bloom remind you of God's new life.

ADDITIONAL REFERENCES
Psalm 40:3; Lamentations 3:22–23

51

Now I Lay Me Down to Sleep

But you are a shield around me, O LORD; you bestow glory on me and lift up my head. To the LORD I cry aloud, and he answers me from his holy hill. I lie down and sleep; I wake again, because the LORD sustains me.

—Psalm 3:3–5

A WEEK AFTER Hurricane Katrina, my husband returned to New Orleans to help with relief efforts at our church. Since there was no place for the children and me to live, we remained in Florida near my parents. Our son, Levi, was two years old at the time, and I didn't realize the impact that our separation would have on him. Once my husband returned to New Orleans, Levi began having night terrors.

Since night terrors involve vivid dreams often accompanied by screaming and crying, though the sufferer is still asleep, they are frightening to anyone involved. My little one would wake in the night, screaming inconsolably. He called for his daddy over and over again. I tried everything I knew to help my little boy. I tried waking him, sleeping with him, playing soft music, and holding and rocking him. After two virtually sleepless months, our family was finally reunited in New Orleans.

Back in the same home with his father, my son's nights became peaceful again. How thankful I was to get to sleep again! Now, if he cries out in the night, his daddy is there to reassure him. Levi is four now, and with every bedtime, I am reminded of the nights with no sleep and what a difference my husband makes in my son's sense of peace.

Our Father God, likewise, offers us peace in frightening times. Knowing our Father is present with us and has everything under control gives us a special sense of security. Just as I wouldn't want to go back to those nights when Levi struggled in fear, I wouldn't want to go back to life the way it was before experiencing the security of my heavenly Father's presence. The same way my son feels peace and safety in his daddy's presence, I feel peace and safety as I abide in the presence of my Father God. My head falls on my pillow each night in peace, and I rest in the security God brings to me.

Prayer: *Lord, I will lie down in peace and sleep, trusting You to care for me.*

Gentle Breeze: Tonight as you go to bed, read Psalm 3:3–5 and use it as a good night prayer to God.

ADDITIONAL REFERENCES
Hebrews 4:9–10; Matthew 11:28–29

52

The Voice of Encouragement

Just before dawn Paul urged them all to eat. "For the last fourteen days," he said, "you have been in constant suspense and have gone without food—you haven't eaten anything. Now I urge you to take some food. You need it to survive. Not one of you will lose a single hair from his head." After he said this, he took some bread and gave thanks to God in front of them all. Then he broke it and began to eat. They were all encouraged and ate some food themselves.

—ACTS 27:33–36

DURING THE AFTERMATH and recovery from natural disaster, fatigue and depression are rampant among disaster victims and relief workers. Days pass with no opportunity to rest and no end in sight. Giving in to discouragement and exhaustion is easy, especially when communication is limited and relief efforts are slow. Often, regular meals are neglected, healthy rest periods are abandoned, and physical breakdown adds to the emotional strain of disaster.

Paul had ridden out a terrible storm on a ship full of soldiers and prisoners. The men had been fighting for survival for two weeks. Paul kept his morale up by communicating with God. He then began to instruct and encourage the others, reassuring them of God's plan. He also gave thought to the practical, urging the men to eat and keep up their strength.

In times of hardship, God usually sends someone to be His voice of reason and reassurance. Could you be His voice to those around you? Stay connected with the Lord, stay calm, and be willing to let Him speak words of comfort through you.

Prayer: Lord, I am willing to be Your messenger of encouragement. Show me how to lift up those around me.

Gentle Breeze: Find someone who needs words of encouragement, and be the one to share them!

⌒

ADDITIONAL REFERENCES
Judges 20:22; Acts 9:31; Acts 15:32

53

Just in Time

But those who wait on the LORD shall renew their strength;
they shall mount up with wings like eagles, they shall run
and not be weary, they shall walk and not faint.
—Isaiah 40:31 (NKJV)

I PEELED MY screaming son off of me and handed him to the waiting preschool teacher. I bravely turned and walked down the sidewalk, but didn't make it to my van before the tears started. We had been displaced for three weeks because of Hurricane Katrina. My husband had returned to New Orleans to work, but the children and I were in Florida on our own. I had returned to my former job at an insurance agency since we had no idea what our financial situation would be in the coming months. The unwelcome changes had worn me down. I called my husband in despair. "I'm not so sure I can do this anymore," I cried. "I know we thought God wanted us to return to New Orleans, but now I just don't know if I can hold up under all this."

With no end to our separation in sight, since housing in New Orleans was extremely difficult to come by, my husband and I shared a sad conversation. He tried to comfort me and encourage me to stay hopeful. He felt sure we were doing what God wanted us to do, but he couldn't help being shaken by my doubts. We hung up with no resolution, and my tears kept coming. I went about my day with a weary heaviness over me.

Later that evening, my husband called. "Tell me this isn't what God wants us to do!" he exclaimed. He proceeded to inform me that someone, a stranger, had come to our church that day and asked him if we needed anything. Half jokingly, he had said, "I need a place to live so I can bring my family home," thinking that request was for the impossible. But the reply, "I'll be back," surprised him.

The stranger came back a few hours later with the best news we had heard in three weeks! He had a personal friendship with an apartment complex manager and had persuaded that friend to rent an apartment to us if we could come with a deposit right away. Of course, my husband had gone directly to the apartment complex and completed our application. He was calling to tell me that we had secured an apartment at a complex just two miles from our church!

Getting that apartment in such an ideal location was a true miracle. Somehow, we had bypassed a waiting list of more than 300 and now had a place to live! Though the move-in date was several weeks away, we finally had a light at the end of our tunnel. Just as I was about to give up, God had orchestrated a solution for us. I believe God timed His provision in the way that He knew would show me clearly how He was caring for my family and me. If you are waiting for God to move, take heart. He will be there just in time.

Prayer: Lord, *help me trust You. Help me patiently wait for Your perfect timing.*

Gentle Breeze: When I was a teenager, we put red dot stickers on our watches to remind us of Jesus' sacrifice for us. Try placing a small sticker on your watch to remind you that you're on God's timetable.

ADDITIONAL REFERENCES
Esther 4:14; Psalm 31:15; Psalm 62:8

54

Spread the Fragrance

But thanks be to God, who always leads us in triumphal procession in Christ and through us spreads everywhere the fragrance of the knowledge of him.

—2 CORINTHIANS 2:14

SMELLS HAVE A profound effect on the human brain. Certain scents can trigger memories, emotions, and even physical responses. My favorite scented candle is sold only during the fall. I always buy several so I will be able to enjoy their comforting smell throughout the year. My husband still wears the same cologne he wore when we first married years ago. The scent always makes me smile and reminds me of good times we've had together. After Hurricane Katrina, the different smells were signals of the awful destruction that had taken place. The stench of mold, chemical spills, stagnant water, and death lingered for months in some areas of the city.

At the time Paul wrote 2 Corinthians 2:14, the smell of incense was associated with victory after a battle. The winning army would return home in a great procession as the people ahead of them would shake incense burners. The smell of victory would draw a great crowd to the parade.

When we know God, His presence in our lives is similar to the smell of incense ahead of a victory procession. When He lives through us, others are drawn to Him through us. They notice the peace and joy in our lives and want to share in the victory.

I find it interesting that the fragrance of the victory incense was spread by burning and shaking. Many times I've resisted that in my life. I didn't realize that those times of brokenness allowed God's presence to shine through more powerfully.

With Jesus in our lives, we are always in a victory parade. Let's continue to be instruments through whom He spreads His fragrance.

Prayer: Dear God, spread Your beautiful scent to others through me.

Gentle Breeze: Take a few moments to enjoy one of your favorite scents. Let the comfort of that smell remind you of God's presence in your life.

ADDITIONAL REFERENCES
Psalm 45:4; Psalm 44:7; 1 Corinthians 15:57

55

Free to All

*For there is no difference between Jew and Gentile—the
same Lord is Lord of all and richly blesses all who call on
him, for, "Everyone who calls on the name of the Lord
will be saved."*

—ROMANS 10:12–13

AFTER A DISASTER, Red Cross lines fill with people from all
walks of life. Those whose paths would normally never cross stand
together in the same situation. No amount of money or prestige
exempts anyone from the pain of natural disaster, and no one
can lay low enough in the depths of society to escape it. In the
time of immediate need after a devastating storm or fire, help is
offered to all. No one is turned away because of job, wealth, skin
color, or religious affiliation. Within the state of emergency, we
witness a level playing field, where pain is shared by all and help
is extended to all who ask.

God's grace has no regard for social status. He saves everyone
who calls to Him. No one will ever have enough money to buy
God's love. No one will ever have so little that he or she receives His
mercy based on poverty. His grace is freely given to all, regardless of
financial status, cultural group, occupation, or family heritage. We
all owed an enormous debt to God, but Jesus paid that debt when
He died in our place. That's why we can't earn God's acceptance; it
has already been purchased for us.

Have you stood before God and accepted the free gift of His
love? He holds His grace out as a gift to you. All you have to do
is receive it. Will you?

*Prayer: Jesus, I need Your grace. I surrender my life to You, knowing
that You are my only way to a life lived in right standing with God.*

Gentle Breeze: Draw a red cross somewhere visible, and let it remind you of God's free gift.

ADDITIONAL REFERENCES
John 3:16–17; Romans 6:23

56

Push the Button

*You will keep in perfect peace him whose mind is steadfast,
because he trusts in you.*

—Isaiah 26:3

ON A VISIT to New Orleans, my parents brought to my son, Levi, a red fire engine with plenty of buttons and noises. The truck was a big hit with Levi, especially one particular button. He must have pushed that button at least a hundred times in the first hour or two he had the truck. When we could no longer stand the noise of the fire engine, we went as far as to hide it for a while.

Levi's favorite button on that engine served as a reminder to me one particularly stressful day as I threw myself across my bed in frustration. God's Word became the button I pushed as I opened my Bible, hoping to find a passage that would help me calm down and refocus.

Isaiah 26:3 provided the reminder I needed. As I moved my thoughts back to my Savior and what He has asked me to do, a happy, peaceful feeling came over me. It was the perfect peace that comes from pushing the same old button again.

After Hurricane Katrina, most of our children's toys were lost. But my husband saved the red fire engine. New batteries were put in, and my son was able to push its buttons again. As soon as we turned on the fire engine, guess which button he pushed? He, of course, pushed that same old favorite we'd heard so many times before. I'm still reminded by Levi's fire engine that when life lets me down, that one button of hope in God works every time.

Life will often bring along circumstances to distract us from the ministry God has called us to do. When we begin to get distracted, spending a few moments focusing on God's Word helps redirect our thoughts to be on Him.

May you and I take a tip from Levi and his repetitive button pushing. Let's hang on to the Lord, and push that button of hope in God over and over, keeping our minds steadfast.

Prayer: *Prince of Peace, thank You for always being here for me. Help me keep my mind focused on You.*

Gentle Breeze: Form the habit of reading Scripture each day.

~

ADDITIONAL REFERENCES
Psalm 119:105; Psalm 119:114; John 1:14

57

Reliable Love

And so we know and rely on the love God has for us. God is love. Whoever lives in love lives in God, and God in him.

—1 JOHN 4:16

OUR ELEVENTH WEDDING anniversary was spent traveling from Florida to New Orleans. "I'm sorry we aren't celebrating today," my husband said. "We'll have a date night later this week."

After a few days, I began to wonder if this anniversary would be overlooked. I am blessed to have an attentive, romantic guy who doesn't normally let anniversaries go unnoticed. Right when I was ready to send him a subtle reminder, he called me from work to let me know he had scheduled a babysitter for our anniversary dinner. I couldn't help but grin like a teenager. I should have known my sweet husband still had me on his heart.

As our marital relationship deepens each year, I not only have the privilege of knowing my husband's love, but I can also rely on his love. Our 11 years of marriage have been full of ups and downs. We have already fulfilled the "for better or worse" part of our vows. And on the other side of "worse," we have found that deep, reliable love. No matter what may happen out in the world, we can come home to unconditional acceptance and love.

Reliable love is what sustained us through the disaster of Katrina and through my serious health problems. This incredible love comes directly from God. His presence in our marriage is the source of our love. We can love each other freely because God has loved us with an overwhelming love that is steady and sure.

God has this same love for you. As life goes on, you can not only know God's love, but you can count on it. No matter what you are facing, you can go on with courage, knowing that you are passionately loved by our God.

Prayer: Loving God, help me to love others with Your dependable love.

Gentle Breeze: Take some time to dwell on God's love for you.

⁓

ADDITIONAL REFERENCES
Exodus 15:13; Psalm 33:22; Ephesians 3:17–19

58

Urgent Pleas

O LORD, I call to you; come quickly to me. Hear my voice when I call to you. May my prayer be set before you like incense; may the lifting up of my hands be like the evening sacrifice.

—PSALM 141:1–2

THERE IS NO urgency like that of a mother who is frightened for the safety of her children. Martha Rogers left two of her sons at an aunt's house in Warren, Arkansas. She and her husband drove about 25 miles through a severe storm to stay at his parents' home for the night. Once they reached their destination, they tried to call the boys, but could not get through. Then a news bulletin flashed on the TV screen, reporting a tornado had hit Warren and caused considerable damage. Panic followed as Martha and her husband drove frantically back to Warren, praying for their sons. They were stopped by police officers outside of Warren and told that no one was being allowed in except for emergency personnel. Martha pleaded with the officer, explaining that her children were there. Her tears were to no avail. The officer told her, "If they're hurt, they'll be taken care of. If not, you'll find out tomorrow or the next day."

Martha spent a long night waiting to hear about her sons. Her only option was to cry out to the Lord for help. The next afternoon brought good news as she was able to return to Warren, where her sons were waiting with no injuries. Two doors down from where the boys had been, a house was completely gone. All along the block, homes had rooms torn away or were twisted on their foundations. Martha knew God had protected her boys.

Some moments in life we are left, as Martha was, with no option but to cry out to God. In those times, we can candidly share with Him our deepest pain. God is not uncomfortable with our desperate, honest prayers. In fact, in our most desperate times, we find ourselves climbing up into our Father's lap more often than usual. There we begin an intimacy with our God that comes no other way. Today, your desperate pleas are heard and understood by our Lord. He hears even the cries that we ourselves are embarrassed to express. Don't be afraid to let Him hear you pour out your pain.

Prayer: *Father, I'm so glad You are not uncomfortable with hearing my real feelings. You are not intimidated by my cries. Hear my deepest needs today.*

Gentle Breeze: Consider the candidness of your prayers. Are you sharing your true heart with God? Try telling God something honest today.

ADDITIONAL REFERENCES
Psalm 139:1; Psalm 34:17; Luke 18:6–8

59

Time to Trust

Trust in the LORD with all your heart and lean not on your own understanding.
—PROVERBS 3:5

WHEN I RECEIVED the news that my dad would need emergency open-heart surgery, Proverbs 3:5 came to mind immediately. I had known the verse since I had been a child. I had trusted the Lord for financial provision when my husband was in Bible college. I had trusted God's leading when we left college to take a ministry position in our hometown.

Now I had an opportunity to trust the Lord again—this time with my daddy's life. Trusting the Lord with all my heart meant literally placing my dad's heart in God's hands.

God proved Himself completely trustworthy. He brought comfort and hope to my family and me during the frightening time of my dad's heart surgery. God's presence enabled us to endure the stress of those difficult days.

Though I could not understand why my family faced that difficult time, I was comforted knowing nothing is too big for God. Our scare with Dad's heart gave us an opportunity to put "feet" on our trust in God. We surrendered to the Lord and rested in the peace of knowing He was in control. Trusting God through my dad's health problems gave way to a natural trust in God through the frightening experience of Hurricane Katrina. We had great peace through the ordeal, knowing that we had trusted God before and Katrina would be no different.

I'm so glad that when my understanding runs out, and even before, God can be trusted to handle my situation. Trust Him with all your heart for whatever you face today.

Prayer: *Thank You, Father, that I can trust You with all my heart.*

Gentle Breeze: As you walk outside today, notice all God has created that is beyond our understanding. Enjoy knowing you can trust Him with situations you do not understand.

ADDITIONAL REFERENCES
Psalm 9:10; Psalm 13:5; 1 Peter 2:6

60

Surrender Your Loss

Therefore, I urge you, brothers, in view of God's mercy, to offer your bodies as living sacrifices, holy and pleasing to God—this is your spiritual act of worship.

—ROMANS 12:1

AFTER TWO MONTHS of displacement because of Hurricane Katrina, it was time to return to New Orleans. God had worked miracles in our lives by providing for our every need since the storm. During displacement, I had the chance to live in my hometown, close to my family. I worked at a job I loved but had left the first time we moved to New Orleans. Now, on top of the pain of Katrina, it was time to say good-bye again to so many people I loved and head back to a broken city. I knew God wanted us to return, and I wanted to follow Him more than anything. I still hurt over having to leave the people who had loved me and comforted me, not only after Katrina, but for most of my life. I was tearing away from my roots again.

As I searched for comfort, I realized the loss I would take for the sake of obedience to God was something I could give to Him in worship. In tears, I began to release my wants to Him. At His feet I laid the sacrifice I made for His sake. I was surprised by the joy I found in making a sacrifice for Him.

I had been given the opportunity to express love to the Lord through costly obedience, and it was an exhilarating experience! Hurt gave way to joy as I began to return love to the One who has showed so much love to me. Only God can turn loss into a new experience of love.

Try turning your loss into an expression of love to Jesus.

Prayer: Precious Friend, You are worthy of more than I could ever give. I place my losses before You as an offering of love.

Gentle Breeze: Take another cheerful step through whatever you are enduring, realizing that as you honor God in this way, you express your love to Him.

ADDITIONAL REFERENCES
Mark 12:33; Philippians 4:6–7; Philippians 3:7–9

LIVE*Chat*

IN THIS BOOK, my story has been shared in pieces, along with stories from other survivors of disasters. Now I'd like to invite you to sit in on a LIVEChat session, a small-group discussion time during which survivors fellowship and encourage one another. I hope this small-group discussion concept will be a useful example to you who are or are working with survivors of natural or other disasters.

Let me explain how LIVEChat came to be and how it works to uplift those who are suffering.

Just before Hurricane Katrina, I had planned to kick off a new small group for women on Wednesday evenings at my church. I wanted to do something simple, casual, and fun for the mothers who were waiting in our church parking lot for their children who were involved in the children's choir. The group was to start the week Katrina hit, so it was obviously delayed. I had no clue at that time how God was preparing me through that small-group idea to help deal with Katrina's disastrous effects.

A few months after the storm, we proceeded with the planned small-group sessions. This simple idea for reaching mothers of children's choir participants became an effective and amazing way for us to deal with the fallout Katrina had left in our lives.

Week by week, our small group met; we called it LIVEChat. As we began to discuss issues surrounding Katrina, our hearts were comforted, new relationships were formed, and we began to look forward to our "safe place" to share struggles each week.

As the group leader, I would choose a discussion topic for each meeting, usually something I knew the group members were dealing with or something that was a hot topic on the news that we were all facing. Each group meeting, I would leave in awe of the way God equipped group members to help one another. I would introduce the topic, and inevitably, a group member would be struggling with that very issue. Then another group member would offer experience, advice, and comfort to the struggling member.

As the weeks passed, I could see that our LIVEChat group had become a real solution for helping the group members deal with the added stress, pain, and depression brought about by Katrina.

We hope that this format will help you, the reader, connect with others in similar, uplifting relationships—whether in a group or one-on-one setting. Whatever you glean from the discussion that follows, the truth is that loving support and dialogue with others prove to be of great comfort during times of struggle. Hopefully, this LIVEChat discussion will provide insight as to how to share comfort with others, the comfort that comes from God alone.

In addition to the LIVEChat discussion, a topical Scripture reference index is provided to help you share God's Word, to help you speak the right word at the right time (Proverbs 25:11).

Now before we get into the discussion, I'd like to introduce to you the real people with other real stories not featured in the earlier readings.

The LIVEChat Ladies

Alesha: A single mother of three boys, Alesha works two jobs. Alesha and her boys stayed with family while they were evacuated.

Carrie: A single seminary student and children's minister, Carrie lived at home with her mother while evacuated and returned to seminary campus as soon as housing reopened in the fall of 2006. She continues to serve the church and the city of New Orleans in ministry.

Christy: A married mother of two children, Christy was pregnant with her first as she evacuated for Katrina. Her daughter was born as the storm hit New Orleans. Since Katrina, Christy and her family have moved into an apartment and have been blessed with a second child, a son.

Danita: A single woman, Danita lives with her sister in their family home in New Orleans. Danita has survived many life-threatening surgeries and deals with limitations due to a birth defect in her hip. Organizing ministry events and serving others in spite of her own pain, Danita has inspired many people in the aftermath of Katrina.

Elise: A single mother of one toddler, Elise began attending LIVEChat after she met Jesus through our church's preschool program, which her son attends. Since Katrina, Elise and her son have settled into a small home, and Elise has secured a job that works well with her schedule as a single mom.

Joann: A single mom of five, Joann has three children under the age of 18 still living at home. She works full-time at a local superstore. I met Joann just as I returned to New Orleans. Since Katrina, she has survived cancer and near homelessness.

Savina: Both a married mother of three grown children and a grandmother, Savina experienced loss through Katrina. She and her husband lost their home in the Chalmette area. Savina, a cardiology technician, returned to her job after Katrina and was finally able to purchase a home near our church.

Susan: A married mother of one, Susan is a kidney transplant recipient who currently awaits another transplant due to complications with her first one. During Katrina, Susan and her husband waited five days for word on their only son's whereabouts and safety, since he had been attending a conference and had to stay stranded in the conference city.

Sample LIVEChat Session

Rebecca: Welcome to LIVEChat. We've all been through Hurricane Katrina and experienced it in different ways. Tonight let's talk about Katrina's effect on our lives and how we've dealt with this experience. I'd like to start by asking, what surprised you the most about how Katrina affected you?

Susan: For me, it was the loss of so many friends. At least four out of five of my closest friends have moved away or didn't come back. All at once, most of my friends were gone. That was a big loss.

Danita: I was surprised because, at the time, I was just coming out of several years of being bedridden. So for me, after the hurricane, I started to do things I never thought I'd be able to do. God really started to speak to me that I needed to help people be prepared for whatever emergency may arise.

Rebecca: And you've done that. You're now planning your second emergency preparedness event.

Danita: Yes. And I was surprised that I was able to do something like that.

Christy: Of course, for me, Sylvia was the biggest surprise of the storm. Her birth date is the day of Katrina, August 29, 2005.

Rebecca: So you had Katrina *and* a brand-new baby to deal with!

Christy: Yes.

Carrie: What surprised me most was not being able to contact anyone. Phone service was down for about two weeks.

Joann: Same with me. My kids were in Mississippi with their father, and I couldn't get through to find out if they were alive or anything. I was a wreck.

Rebecca: I think I was also surprised by having to move. Normally, when we've moved, I have had time to plan and pack and adjust to the idea. I left my home thinking I'd be back in a few days, and I've never gone back to that home. I packed a cooler with milk in it because we had no money, and I had just bought milk. I didn't want my milk to go to waste. So I left my wedding pictures, but I took the milk!

Carrie: Yeah, Becky, do you remember when we finally caught up with each other and you told me about the first Sunday sermon you heard after the storm? The preacher had used the verse, *"Cast your bread upon the waters"* [Ecclesiastes 11:1]. We were laughing because you had left several loaves of bread someone had given you, and you had literally cast your bread upon the water. I remember being back on the seminary campus wondering how that bread must look now.

Rebecca: [*Laughing*] Yes, I'll never forget that Sunday sermon! It was so strange to move. We moved a total of three times after Katrina, and none of it was prepared for. It's a weird feeling to move when you aren't planning to move.

Rebecca: Let's move on to another question: What has helped you the most as you've coped with the disaster?

Danita: God. Definitely my relationship with Jesus and my Christian brothers and sisters.

Susan: I agree. My Christian family has been such a support for me. And my husband—he's been there for me through it all. Also, those who came from all over the country and gave of themselves, stayed here at the church, and just helped however they could.

Savina: For me, it was my co-workers. After the storm, they called me; each doctor I worked for and so many of my co-workers called me to make sure we were all right. They said, "We'll help you get back however we can." When we came back for a visit, they had a huge spread, almost like a reception, and they all said, "Savina, we're so glad you are here." My manager offered me my job back, and many co-workers gave us furniture and a place to stay and helped us get back on our feet while we waited to see what would happen with our house.

Elise: Yes, you really did not have an address anymore, did you?

Savina: No, we literally didn't have an address. It's so good to have an address again…and a church family, after looking so long for something like what we had before the storm.

Joann: This church helped my kids and me so much. After I finally found them and got them back home, things were so rough. But this church was feeding so many people in our neighborhood. Three times a day they would come down our street and knock on the door with food. If it hadn't been for that, my kids and I may have starved to death after the storm. My little girl would look out the window and say, "They'll be comin' soon, Mama." And sure enough, they'd show up every day with food. It's how we found this church and got involved with so many new friends here.

Rebecca: Tell me what you needed the most as you think back on those first days and weeks after the disaster.

Carrie: I needed a way to find the people I had lost! I've already decided we'll never leave again without having every possible contact number for where we might be headed.

Joann: Yes! I needed a reliable way to get in touch with my kids. I needed my kids with me. I'll never let that happen again—separating from them during an evacuation. If we have to evacuate again, they'll be superglued to my side.

Alesha: I had left with only about $100 cash in my wallet. I didn't have my debit card, and I had only one check in my checkbook. I tried to apply for FEMA, and I couldn't get through, so I found a way to get online and apply online. They called me and said they weren't sure I would qualify. I cried! I was away from home and didn't know if I still had a house. I had only $100, and I have three kids. A couple of days later, I got a check from FEMA.

Rebecca: So you're saying you needed information about who to call and what to do to get help?

Alesha: Exactly!

Danita: Everybody needed that information. That's why it's so important to be prepared for an emergency and gather numbers and information ahead of time so that this never happens again.

Susan: I needed medical help. I was supposed to get test results from a kidney biopsy the day after the storm hit. There were no test results, and I ended up in Memphis with doctors who couldn't help me without those results. I had a virus that destroyed my kidney, and I have to be on dialysis now. Even after the storm, I couldn't be around people. I helped in the back with bagging up food and stuff, but I couldn't be around people or the mold because of my health.

Rebecca: What do you miss most from before the storm?

Alesha: I just miss normal life. I mean, it's been two years now, but everything isn't normal. We don't have enough people to work in the stores or hospitals. Everything is different.

Elise: I miss the last letter my dad ever wrote to me. He passed away in 1989. The letter was in our Mississippi home on the coast. When I went over there after the storm, it was as if everything had just been wiped clean away. You couldn't even see where anything used to be. On our property, there were no trees, no buildings left.

Savina: Yes, it's not easy to lose everything at once; and even though you have to get new stuff, none of it feels like yours. It takes a while to get adjusted to even new things. It's not like we had a choice or a chance to plan to replace something we didn't want anymore. Everything familiar was gone and suddenly had to be replaced with all new stuff.

Rebecca: Susan, you brought up earlier all the people that are now gone. I think that's the biggest part of the loss from Katrina—all the people who are no longer here.

Carrie: Yeah. It's not as if we really said good-bye.

Rebecca: Well, most of us expected to be back in a few days. We didn't know we were saying good-bye for good.

Carrie: Yeah, and there's just no closure there. Sometimes I'll walk past my friend's dorm room now and look in there expecting her to be there. I forget that she doesn't live there anymore!

Joann: I miss how people would sometimes smile at you or open the door for you. I work at a store, and these days, people would sooner throw a door at you than open it for you.

Savina: Yes, I think it's brought out a lot of anger in people.

Joann: Yeah, I just miss the way people were. Seems like everybody's always stressed out now.

Rebecca: As we wrap up, tell me how your life has changed for the good because of the disaster.

Joann: I just thank God for my friend from work who told me to come to this church. I've gotten my life on a good track now, and I'm gonna keep going in that direction.

Alesha: It's still a bumpy road sometimes.

Joann: Yeah, there's been plenty of bumps, but I'm so glad I have friends and people now who support me and help me. I know I'm gonna stay in the right direction.

Rebecca: That's awesome!

Savina: Sometimes people come over and just can't believe how we've been able to put this new house together. But God has just provided. Like we needed a two-drawer filing cabinet. I mentioned it to my husband, and the next morning on my way to work, a brand-new filing cabinet was sitting on the side of the road.

I thought for sure it would be full of water or something. But no, someone had just set it out by the road because they didn't want it anymore. That's just one of tons of miracles God has done for us.

Danita: I have a similar story to share. I had evacuated with only a nightgown, but ended up staying in another family's home, and I needed a robe. Because of my size, I wasn't able to get one at the local mission in Texas where we were staying. The lady at the mission said many larger people were needing help, but they rarely got anything for the larger sizes. So I found a way to get online and sent out a message to an organization for larger people that if anyone had extra clothing, to please send it to this mission. The organization ended up contacting me, and people sent me several robes. I had one for me and several to give away!

Susan: Same thing happened to me! I needed a pair of house shoes, but I wear a very odd size, only about a size 2 for women, which is nearly impossible to find. While we were evacuated, I was helping my sister look through some clothes that were given to her, never expecting anything to be there that would fit me. But all of a sudden, I found some brand-new house shoes. And they were blue! I had wanted blue to match my gown and robe. They were my size and fit perfectly.

Savina: It's like God was there saying, "I'm still here. I'm still in control."

Rebecca: Isn't it neat how He reminds us that He's still paying attention, even to the little details, like wanting blue house shoes?

Joann: Yeah, and it's like now I see Him more in other things too.

Rebecca: Exactly. God has shown us parts of Himself that we would never have been able to see except for a disaster. He uses those bad experiences to get our attention and take us to a higher place.

Danita: Yes! When you asked this question, I kept thinking of the Scripture verse that says God works all things together for the good of those who love Him and are called according to His purpose [see Romans 8:28]. It's true. You just have to get past that initial moment of shock to see that God is still there and He's gonna make it all right somehow.

Rebecca: Ladies, I've really enjoyed tonight. Thanks for chatting with me about your experiences.

I hope you enjoyed sitting in on our LIVEChat. In times of need, disaster, or any kind of pain, we all need to know we are not alone. We need the warmth of a friend's embrace and the understanding nod of a like-minded person.

Through the sharing of this LIVEChat, you've been able to get to know a few of the women who have found the support they need each week as they come together to share, encourage, laugh, and learn. More importantly, you've had a chance to meet real women who have survived great disaster. The winds of destruction took much from these women in 2005, but the winds of hope have blown gently in their hearts, bringing healing, friendship, restoration, and renewed laughter to their lives.

Those same winds of hope blow from the heart of Jesus right to you, wherever you are today. Because of Jesus Christ, there is hope in any situation, no matter how desperate it may seem. He gave His very life to purchase the hope of heaven for you, and He lives again to give you the hope of amazing life on earth. Close your eyes, tilt your head back, and let His winds of hope caress your face and your heart.

Topical Scripture Index

THIS INDEX INCLUDES Scripture references that comforted me through the stages of disaster recovery. I've pinpointed different emotions or feelings I experienced and the Scriptures that brought hope and comfort to me as I experienced them.

DEPRESSION

Genesis 16:6–13
Deuteronomy 31:6
Psalm 3:3
Isaiah 41:10
Isaiah 50:7
John 3:16
Romans 8:35–39
1 Corinthians 15:54–57
2 Corinthians 3:17–18
Hebrews 4:14–15
1 John 4:16–18

GRIEF

Psalm 119:165
Isaiah 35:10
John 14:27
1 Corinthians 15:54
Philippians 3:20–21
1 Thessalonians 4:13–14

NEED

Job 36:11
Psalm 3:3

Proverbs 19:23
Matthew 6:28
Matthew 6:31–34
Matthew 10:29–31
2 Corinthians 9:9–11
Ephesians 1:3
Philippians 4:12
Philippians 4:19
Hebrews 13:5

PANIC

Job 26:2
Psalm 56:3
Psalm 91:4
Psalm 121:5
Psalm 147:5
Proverbs 2:8
Proverbs 10:25
Isaiah 35:4
Nahum 1:3
Matthew 7:24–25
Luke 8:25
Philippians 3:21
Philippians 4:7

SADNESS

Job 8:21
Psalm 5:11
Psalm 46:1
Psalm 103:17
Proverbs 15:13
Isaiah 61:3
Matthew 28:20
Romans 5:3
Romans 15:13
Philippians 4:4
1 Peter 3:13–16

SHOCK

Deuteronomy 3:24
Job 26:2
Psalm 71:5
Psalm 112:7
Psalm 119:105
Psalm 147:5
Isaiah 43:19
Isaiah 55:8–11
John 15:7
Acts 9:1–18
Philippians 3:21
Colossians 3:10

STRESS

Psalm 23:3
Psalm 44:3
Psalm 46:10
Psalm 62:5
Psalm 91:1
Psalm 103:5
Isaiah 40:31
Matthew 11:28
John 16:33
1 Corinthians 15:54
2 Corinthians 4:16
Philippians 4:8
1 John 5:3–5

WORRY

Deuteronomy 3:24
Job 5:11
Psalm 4:8
Psalm 71:5
Psalm 121:8
Psalm 139:1–4
Isaiah 55:8–11
Matthew 6:28
Luke 18:1–8
Philippians 4:4
Colossians 3:15

New Hope® Publishers is a division of WMU®,
an international organization that challenges Christian believers
to understand and be radically involved in God's mission.
For more information about WMU, go to www.wmu.com.
More information about New Hope books may be found
at www.newhopepublishers.com. New Hope books
may be purchased at your local bookstore.

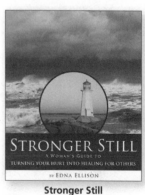